Through the Hitler Line

Memoirs of an Infantry Chaplain

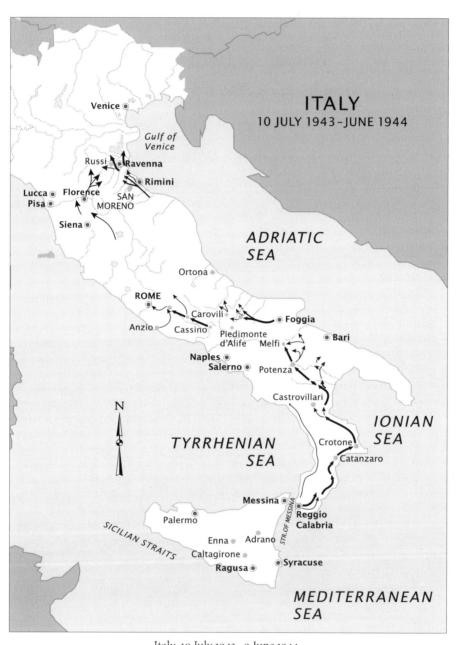

Italy, 10 July 1943 – 9 June 1944

Through the Hitler Line
Memoirs of an Infantry Chaplain

Laurence F. Wilmot

Wilfrid Laurier University Press

We acknowledge the support of the Canada Council for the Arts for our publishing program. We acknowledge the financial support of the Government of Canada through the Book Publishing Industry Development Program for our publishing activities.

National Library of Canada Cataloguing in Publication

Wilmot, Laurence F., 1907–

    Through the Hitler line: memoirs of an infantry chaplain / Laurence F. Wilmot.

(Life writing series)
ISBN 0-88920-426-8

    1. Canada. Canadian Army—Chaplains—Biography. 2. Chaplains, Military—Canada—Biography. 3. World War, 1939–1945—Campaigns—Italy. 4. Canada. Canadian Army. West Nova Scotia Regiment—History. 5. World War, 1939–1945—Personal narratives, Canadian. I. Title. II. Series

D810.C36C39 2003   940.54'78'092   C2003-903074-1

© 2003 Wilfrid Laurier University Press
Waterloo, Ontario, Canada N2L 3C5
www.wlupress.wlu.ca

Cover and text design by P.J. Woodland.

The maps on pages 15, 23, 43, 71, 79, 93 and 109 are reproduced from *The Canadians in Italy 1943–1945,* volume 2 of the *Official History of the Canadian Army in the Second World War,* by Lt.-Col. G.W.L. Nicolson. Maps drawn by Capt. C.C.J. Bond. Ottawa: Queen's Printer, 1956.

Every reasonable effort has been made to acquire permission for copyright material used in this text, and to acknowledge all such indebtedness accurately. Any errors and omissions called to the publisher's attention will be corrected in future printings.

∞
Printed in Canada

No part of this publication may be reproduced, stored in a retrieval system or transmitted, in any form or by any means, without the prior written consent of the publisher or a licence from The Canadian Copyright Licensing Agency (Access Copyright). For an Access Copyright licence, visit www.accesscopyright.ca or call toll free to 1-800-893-5777.

To the glory of God at work
in a world in chaos

and

to the memory of those gallant men of the
West Nova Scotia Regiment with whom it was
my privilege to serve during World War II.
Many of them gave their lives to rescue
from oblivion such civilization as we had
been able to achieve.

Contents

List of Photographs ix

List of Maps x

Foreword xi

Acknowledgements xiii

Introduction xv

Chapter 1 Treading Cautiously into the Unknown 1

Chapter 2 Ministry on the Arielli Front 13

Chapter 3 Taking Up God's Armour 27

Chapter 4 Breaking the Hitler Line 41

Chapter 5 A Tourist in Wartime 59

Chapter 6 Preparing for the Attack 69

Chapter 7 Tragedy at Foglia River 77

Chapter 8 Fierce Fighting and Close Calls 91

Chapter 9 A Time of Stress and a Moment of Rest 101

Chapter 10 Roman Holiday, Russi Road 107

Chapter 11 Prayers for the Fallen 117

Chapter 12 Liberating Holland 129

Chapter 13 The Guns Fall Silent 137

Glossary 145

List of Photographs

page 5
Laurence Wilmot, Swan River, Manitoba, June 1942

page 57
Lt. Col. R.S.E. (Ronnie) Waterman
A Bren gunner at the Hitler Line
Lt. Col. Frank Hiltz
Padre Wilmot with Medical Officer Dr. Hyman Mendelson
Three chaplains examine the steel helmet worn
by Padre Wilmot during the battle of the Hitler Line

page 99
Padre Wilmot seated high up in the Colosseum
At a campsite in a vineyard
West Nova men who were confirmed
by the Bishop of Lichfield at All Saints
Anglican Cathedral, Rome
West Nova officers and a casualty
A tank concealed in a ruined house
The Mortar Platoon of the WNSR at a front-line
open-air shower stall
West Nova Scotia Regiment cemetery,
near San Lorenzo

page 100
A German tank taken by the West Novas
in the Lamone Advance
Lt. Col. A.L. Saunders
Padre Wilmot with his truck

page 100, continued

Col. J.L. Ralston visiting the regiment after
the battle at the Gothic Line

Dedication of the WSNR cemetery at Russi

Padre Wilmot giving the blessing at a farewell service

page 143

Capt. Laurence F. Wilmot at the end of
his military duties, 1945

List of Maps

Southern Italy, p. 15
10 July 1943–9 June 1944

The Adriatic Sector, p. 23
28 November 1943–4 January 1944

The Crossing of the Moro and the Battle for Ortona, p. 23
6 December 1943–4 January 1944

The Breaking of the Gustav and Hitler Lines, p. 43
11–23 May 1944

Northern Italy, p. 71
10 June 1944–25 February 1945

The Breaking of the Gothic Line, p. 79
30 August–3 September 1944

The Advance to Rimini, p. 93
3–22 September 1944

From the Montone to the Senio, p. 109
2 December 1944–5 January 1945

Foreword

I FEEL VERY HONOURED to have been asked to provide a foreword to this book, in my capacity (I suppose) as the last wartime commander of the West Nova Scotia Regiment, although, in truth, the war in Europe was over when I was given command for the happy purpose of bringing the regiment home to Canada. Padre Wilmot arrived at the regiment in February 1944, to face the misery of the Arielli position, while I spent a "comfortable" winter in hospital recovering from flesh wounds incurred in December 1943. I returned to the regiment on May 23, 1944, for the final breakthrough of the Hitler Line, so graphically depicted in this book, but after the battle I was sent to the brigade as Intelligence Officer and did not return to the regiment until January 1945. I relate these events only to show that I did not share first-hand in the major battles otherwise described herein. It was not long, however, before I heard of the remarkably courageous activities of the padre of the West Novas, and I had occasion to view the shell-torn helmet that evidenced at least one of his almost miraculous escapes from death.

Some padres may have been content to remain out of the immediate battle; to tend to the wounded brought in from the field; and to bury those who were killed. In fairness, this is what they were often expected, or even ordered, to do. But Laurie Wilmot was of a different ilk. He was bound to join the soldiers in their most forward positions in and out of battle, to render what physical and spiritual assistance he could in the most dire perils.

This is a book about war and great courage, but it is, above all, a story of great faith; of a priest who each morning put his life into the hands of his God, willing to face without flinching the greatest dangers that might befall him. Those who read his story will grasp some measure of that faith and the protecting presence of God in all of life.

Padre Wilmot humbly wears the Military Cross for his great bravery in the approaches to the Gothic Line defences, but anyone with an understanding of his exploits in the Hitler Line battles must feel, as I do, that no braver hero could merit the highest Canadian award for valour, the Victoria Cross.

Harry M. Eisenhauer,
Major (Retired)
Calgary, Alberta

Acknowledgements

Many of my friends, including former officers and other ranks of the West Nova Scotia Regiment, have urged me to write a memoir of my experience as a regimental chaplain in Italy during World War II. This is the result.

Major Harry M. Eisenhauer of Calgary, Alberta, who served as a platoon commander throughout the Liri Valley battles and subsequently as Brigade Intelligence Officer, and who brought the regiment back to Canada as its commanding officer, has kindly written the foreword.

Major R.G. (Bill) Thexton, CD, of Wolfville, Nova Scotia, who commanded A Company during most of my time with the regiment, assisted me by obtaining copies of regimental and brigade diaries, and generously permitted me to use material from his memoirs, *Times to Remember,* particularly for background information in our approach to the Gothic Line battles and the battles for San Lorenzo and San Fortunato Ridge. He has also written the introduction to my account.

Colonel C. Roger MacLellan, MC, CD, of Kentville, Nova Scotia, Honorary Colonel of the West Nova Scotia Regiment, has gone through the document and carefully checked my use of military terms; and, with the cooperation of Dr. Don I. Rice, CM, of Willowdale, Ontario, who served as a captain and company commander during my time with the regiment, he has made many suggestions to clarify the record and prepare it for publication. Colonel MacLellan has also prepared a glossary of military terms and abbreviations that will be most helpful to readers unfamiliar with military terminology and procedures. I owe these men special thanks for their generous assistance.

My decision to join the Chaplain Service at age thirty-five must have been a signal of doom to my wife, Hope, and our three small children: Laurence Sydney, who was nine years old at the time, Frances Mary Louise, seven, and Hope Fairfield, two. Although it seemed necessary on my part, it was still a wrenching decision for me to make. I am most thankful that Hope accepted the situation with her usual devotion. She and the children joined me at most of my postings in Canada. After saying goodbye to my family in Brockville, Ontario, I sailed on the Queen Elizabeth from Halifax. Hope wrote to me, and prayed for me every day while I was overseas, thus sustaining and inspiring me to press on with my task. After the war, we had a long and eventful life of ministry together until her death on July 2, 1986. My gratitude for her devotion is beyond bounds.

I am also indebted to my second wife, Grace, whom I married on January 21, 1995. We have had wonderful years of companionship together, with the result that I have found the energy and leisure time to bring this material together and, with the assistance of my friends mentioned above, prepare it for publication.

Laurence F. Wilmot
Ex-Padre
West Nova Scotia Regiment
Winnipeg, Manitoba

Introduction

The events described in this book took place many years ago, during the Italian Campaign of World War II in 1943–45. Most of these events, and the only ones on which I am qualified to comment, concern the author's service as chaplain with an infantry battalion in the 1st Canadian Infantry Division.

In February 1944, Laurence Wilmot was posted to the West Nova Scotia Regiment, which was then holding the line some two miles north of the seaport town of Ortona, Italy. Ortona had recently fallen to the Canadians after an epic and costly battle with the German 1st Parachute Division. The weather there was dismal—cold and wet, with snow on the ground. For troops occupying slit trenches all night, it could hardly have been worse. In addition, the junior officers and men in the rifle companies were constantly out on tough fighting patrols to probe the enemy lines, and casualties in the regiment had been heavy. The sound of artillery fire, both enemy and our own, was almost continuous. The crump of mortars and the chatter of machine guns added to the crescendo of noise. It was under these conditions that Laurence Wilmot began his service as chaplain with the West Nova Scotia Regiment.

I happened to be at Rear Battalion Headquarters, situated in a damaged building called Casa Berardi in the hamlet of Berardi, when Laurie arrived. At the time, a few of us were saying farewell to Maj. Al Rogers, who was leaving the battalion for a period of rest after many months in the field as a company commander. I took this opportunity to introduce Laurie to Al and to the others gathered for the occasion. We were as pleased to welcome our new padre as we were sorry to see Al go.

Few that evening could have imagined how fortunate we were in having Laurie Wilmot join us. His warmth, common sense, and strong Christian faith soon made him welcome with the officers and the men alike. Later on, his actions in helping to care for the wounded and evacuate them to safety, often under fire, are described in modest detail in this book.

For much of Laurie's service with the West Novas, our commanding officer was Ronald Waterman. Ronnie was born in England and had joined the Canadian Army in peacetime as a private soldier. In December of 1943, in the rank of lieutenant colonel, he had taken command of the West Nova

Scotia Regiment. It is interesting to read how the commanding officer gradually came to appreciate Laurie's worth until, towards the end, he would consult him regularly on the state of morale, and other matters of importance in the day-to-day life of the regiment.

In this book Laurie also describes in some detail his visits to Rome, including a meeting with Pope Pius XII; to the lost city of Pompeii; and to Assisi, long associated with St. Francis.

This book will be of interest to military historians, and also to those who participated in the Italian Campaign. It might usefully be included as required reading for all appointed to the Canadian Chaplain Service.

Today, nearly sixty years after the events told in this book, Laurence Wilmot, now in his nineties, still maintains a close association with the West Nova Scotia Regiment. He regularly flies from his home in Winnipeg to be with his old soldiers and participate in their reunions, often leading the memorial services.

To them he is, and always will be, their beloved padre.

> Robert G. Thexton
> Major (Retired)
> West Nova Scotia Regiment
> September 1940 – November 1944
> Wolfville, Nova Scotia

Chapter One

Treading Cautiously into the Unknown
September 1939 – January 1944
Canada / Britain / Algeria / Italy

On September 1, 1939, my wife, Hope, and I were in northern Manitoba to attend the official opening of a new highway from Mafeking to The Pas, a major construction job at the time. At the time, I was a travelling (missionary) priest in the Anglican diocese of Brandon, with headquarters in Swan River, Manitoba, and during the years of construction I had held several services for the work crew during the winter months, hence our interest in the completed project. Late on the evening of September 2, I turned on the radio in our hotel room to hear George VI announce to the people of the Commonwealth and all the Western world that Great Britain and France were now, on the morning of September 3 in England, at war with Germany. The declaration of war did not come as a surprise.

Before accepting the appointment as travelling priest I had served for four years (1935–38) as rector of the parish of St. James, Swan River, which included St. Paul's, Bowsman, St. Matthews, Minitonas, and a small mission point at the east end of Swan River Valley that met in Renwer School. I was also rural dean, and oversaw all Anglican work in the valley and points north to Mafeking. Swan River Valley was a flourishing agricultural community. It had been settled during the latter decades of the nineteenth and the early twentieth century, and much of its population was European-born. My congregation at Renwer embraced members of the United, Presbyterian, Lutheran, and Anglican churches, and during our time together we built a church. They were disturbed by the emergence and rapid rise of Hitler and the Nazi regime in Germany and with what was happening to their relatives back home.

A vivid illustration of the impact that events in Europe were having upon the community was provided in the small village of Minitonas, where there were seven Baptist churches, each of a different national origin. When the Sudetenland was taken from Czechoslovakia and given to Germany at the Munich conference, the Royal Canadian Mounted Police had to intervene to prevent bloodshed, and later, when the German juggernaut invaded Poland, they had to break up a battle between the Polish and German Baptists armed with pitchforks.

European affairs had a very different effect on one of my parishioners at Renwer. It was my policy to visit members of the congregation in their homes. On one occasion in the summer of 1938, I called upon a prominent member of the Lutheran Church, a local farmer named Sandy who also operated a sawmill in the Duck Mountains. Born in Germany, he immigrated to Canada with his parents in 1903, and had grown up in the Swan River Valley. Sandy knew me well enough to confide in me, and he opened up with a bitter complaint about the manner in which Hitler was being criticized. He was convinced that Hitler was the greatest statesman to emerge in Europe in centuries and that he was rescuing Germany from ruin. After pouring out his soul, Sandy asked me to explain why other leaders were so critical of Hitler. I responded, "Well, Sandy, I would be glad to discuss this with you, but I suggest that if you really want to know what is behind it all you should tune in to the British Broadcasting Corporation. They are reading Hitler's book, *Mein Kampf,* chapter by chapter in the German language, and discussing its implications. I will drop in one day next week and we can discuss the matter again."

Sandy had a powerful short-wave radio and had been in the habit of tuning in daily to broadcasts from Germany by Hitler and his followers. I called in a week later to find Sandy most apologetic and grateful for my advice. He had done as I suggested and now clearly realized Hitler's viciousness and his threat to world peace. He had already pulled his two teenage sons and a young daughter out of the *Bunds,* or German youth groups, to which they had been recruited by an organization in the valley. It became very evident to me that Sandy was by no means alone in thinking that Hitler had something to offer the rest of the world. Many people of German origin throughout the valley belonged to organizations that worked to pass his way of thinking on to the younger generation.

During the summer of 1938, my last as rector of the parish of Swan River, I introduced a program of Saturday-evening open-air services on a vacant square in the centre of the town. The object of the program was to provide an opportunity for me to speak to the crowds of people who came to town and milled about the streets. I spoke on the theme of "Civilization and Liberty," and interpreted the situation developing in Europe and its implications for all freedom-loving people anywhere in the world, including ourselves. The services were well attended, but I later learned that one prominent Anglican woman complained about them as being un-

Anglican. This was one of the reasons why the bishop had transferred me to the post of travelling priest.

I was transferred to a much wider field that included isolated communities throughout the valley and along the railway north to Mafeking, and three additional congregations along the Hudson's Bay Railway, including Cormorant, the gold-mining town of Herb Lake, and Wabowden, for a total of thirty-five congregations. Most of them were receiving regular pastoral care from the bishop's Messengers of St. Faith's, and I endeavoured to hold a communion service for them once a month. However, I could go only twice a year, at Christmas and Easter, to those along the Hudson's Bay Railway. Services throughout this wider field were well attended and I brought to them the latest developments in Europe and the implications for all who believed in freedom and justice in the world. It was evident to all who were following events in Europe that Hitler would be satisfied with nothing less than world conquest. So the king's message on the evening of September 2, 1939, that England and France were at war with Germany, did not come as a surprise. I recognized that within a matter of days Canada and the people of the Commonwealth would be involved and that the lives of every man, woman, and child would be affected by this dramatically changed situation.

It had been evident for several months that war was imminent. Hitler had ignored the firm ultimatum that France and England had imposed on him on learning that German troops had rolled into Poland. As I said my prayers that night, I realized that my life, too, would soon be changed and that I would also be involved in the struggle.

During the next few months it became evident that my ministry to the scattered congregations in the northern missionary areas of Manitoba was just so much crying in the dark as long as the Nazis remained undefeated. Hitler had issued a challenge to the whole of the Western world that he and his "master race" were determined to demonstrate that our "decadent" civilization was barren and ready for replacement by a "purer" stock which was prepared to enforce its will upon Europe and the world.

That same year, in his Christmas message to the people of Great Britain and the Commonwealth, the king quoted from the little-known poem, "God Knows," by M. Louise Haskins:

> And I said to the man who stood at the gate of the year: "Give me a light that I may tread safely into the unknown."
> And he replied:
> "Go out into the darkness and put your hand into the Hand of God. That shall be to you better than light and safer than the known way."

The essence of the king's message was that the future held a dark prospect indeed, for neither Britain nor the members of the Commonwealth were ready for total war, but must now face just that, and be prepared to give everything they had to defeat this entrenched enemy of mankind.

By April 1940 I was determined to offer my services as an army chaplain. Having had four years of training in the Canadian Officers Training Corps, I had been commissioned as a lieutenant in the Canadian militia during my years at university. Several of my friends who had been serving as chaplains to militia units in larger towns had already been called up and were on their way overseas. This was a difficult decision because I was married and had three children, the youngest, Hope Fairfield, having been born February 19, 1940. Nevertheless, I realized that I could not honestly evade offering my services because of my association with so many members of the militia.

Before making my final decision, I discussed the whole question with the bishop, the Right Reverend W.W.H. Thomas, and told him of the inner promptings that kept irritating my conscience. I requested that he release me so that I could offer myself for service as a chaplain. The bishop was very critical of my desire to go into the service. In his view, those men who had given up their parish responsibilities to enlist were simply seeking adventure and escape from the acknowledged difficulties of a rural ministry. Several of those who had enlisted were already disillusioned to discover that the military had no interest in them or their message. The military considered the clergy and their pastoral services an unnecessary nuisance and interference in the real job of waging war. The bishop urged me to understand that the work in which I was engaged was essential to the real welfare of the country, and to forget the idea of enlisting and carry on with missionary work in the northern part of the diocese.

I realized that the bishop was experiencing difficulties in finding clergy suitable and willing to continue rural missionary work. But I had already served in the diocese for nine years and was now into my second year of travelling missionary work. I had already declined two offers from parishes in Winnipeg because I had promised to serve under the bishop for five years in return for financial assistance with college. For each year of training he had paid $150 towards my tuition. I had been successful in all aspects of my work throughout that time and was at a point in my ministry when I expected some recognition, yet none had come.

In fact, in the summer of 1939 I learned that two important parishes in the diocese had requested permission to offer me a rectorship, an appointment to either of which would have constituted a promotion. The bishop turned down their requests without telling me, and I only learned about them much later from members of the parishes concerned. Earlier in the

Laurence Wilmot, Swan River, Manitoba, June 1942.

fall of 1938, I organized a team ministry for the Swan River Valley with my friend, the Reverend William Hunter, which enabled us to share a variety of ministerial functions throughout the Valley. I had felt obliged to turn down a firm invitation from a parish in Winnipeg because of my involvement in this. A few weeks later the bishop informed me that he was transferring me to the travelling ministry. I accepted his decision, but felt frustrated. I had now come to believe that I had fulfilled all my obligations to the diocese and its bishop. Consequently, at the conclusion of the bishop's lecture, I reiterated my conviction that God was calling me to offer myself for active service in the Canadian Chaplain Service and that I felt I must do this forthwith.

On my return home from that meeting, I wrote to the Principal Protestant Chaplain, the Right Reverend G.A. Wells, who had been warden of St. John's College and under whom I had trained for the ministry, offering my services as a chaplain. I received an affirmative reply. He instructed me to go before the Army Medical Board at Military District No. 10, in Winnipeg, and if accepted, hold myself in readiness to be called up. This I did without delay and awaited developments. To my great disappointment, no offer of appointment came, even though a number of men from the diocese of Brandon were called up, some of whom had scarcely been ordained the required number of years to qualify. I carried on with my travelling work and Hope and I together attended classes for certification in first aid with the St. John Ambulance. We were taught to wrap bandages and splint fractured limbs by two doctors who were veterans of World War 1. These skills were to prove invaluable on the battlefield.

In the summer of 1941 I was interviewed by the head of the newly established Army Personnel Department, who declared his readiness to give me an appointment. I pondered this a while. Finally, in April 1942, I wrote to the Principal Chaplain for an explanation of the long delay. He replied that he had no control over the situation. The board kept a list of men from each diocese in Canada who had offered their services. When a man volunteered for a chaplaincy appointment, his name went to the bottom of the list and gradually, as appointments were made, rose to the top. In my case the bishop kept inserting names above my own, and unless I could deal with the situation at my end there was little he could do to change it.

I wrote to the bishop reporting the information I had received, and then went to see him. I advised him that if he didn't release me, I would resign from the diocese where I had now served for more than ten years. As a matter of fact, I had already been accepted into the Personnel Department of the army as a psychologist, although this was not the position I wished. So, having made myself perfectly clear in my conversation with the bishop, I decided to await results.

Early in June 1942 I received a letter informing me of my appointment as a chaplain. Included were a railway ticket and instructions to proceed to Montreal on July 1. I was to reside in the Drummond Street YMCA and serve a number of small detachments, including the Royal Canadian Ordnance Corps, Royal Canadian Army Service Corps, a downtown drop-in centre for military personnel, two hospitals, and two prisons. I was also to serve as chaplain to the 2nd Battalion, Black Watch Royal Highland Regiment. I met with soldiers of the Ordnance and Army Service Corps and spoke to them during their noon-hour breaks, made regular evening calls at the drop-in centre, and accompanied the Black Watch on a Saturday exercise each week, thus getting to know them. It was a busy summer. In early

August, the Black Watch called me as their chaplain and I joined them in Sussex, New Brunswick. In October I accompanied them to Halifax where they were on coastal defence duty throughout the winter of 1942–43.

In August 1943, I was attached as one of three chaplains—the others were Roman Catholic and United—to No. 2 Canadian General Hospital, which was formed at St. Mary's College, Brockville, Ontario, and in September boarded the *Queen Elizabeth* to proceed overseas. On our arrival in England, No. 2 Canadian General Hospital took over a large military hospital at Bramshott, near Hazelmere, Buckinghamshire. The hospital already had about a thousand military patients when No. 2 Canadian took it over. We three chaplains decided that, prior to our disembarkation leave, we would spend at least two weeks organizing our work and familiarizing ourselves with staff and patients.

Soon after this I had occasion to visit the Senior Chaplain's office in London. I still hankered to serve with men in the field, and so I inquired about the possibility of being posted to a regiment, only to be informed that there were no vacancies in England at that time. I was also told that, in any case, the Anglican Church had more than its share of chaplains already attached to units and any vacancy would be offered to a chaplain of a different denomination. The office advised me to tackle the job that I had in the hospital for at least the forthcoming winter, and this I agreed to do. I accepted the rank of Education Officer at the administrator's request and settled down to work.

Early in November my fellow chaplains went off on their disembarkation leave while I remained, planning to take my leave on their return. I had purchased a new officer's shoulder bag in London and, as I would not be requiring it while they were away, loaned it to Silcox, the United Church padre, who lacked one. They both left on the first Sunday in November. At 1300 hours on Monday the phone rang in the corridor outside my office door. Being the lone chaplain on duty, I answered it, to be greeted by an authoritative voice that declared: "Hello, this is the Senior Chaplain calling from London. May I speak with Honorary Captain Laurence F. Wilmot?" I replied, "This is Captain Wilmot speaking." "Captain Wilmot, you realize you are expected at Blackdown this afternoon at 1600 hours, don't you!" To which I replied, "No, I do not. As a matter of fact, I have an important meeting this evening with a group of patients who were confirmed yesterday, and I am preparing them for their first communion." "Captain Wilmot, you are expected at Blackdown this afternoon. Now, you are not going to let us down, are you?" I again replied, "Does this mean bag and baggage?" The reply: "I suggest you bring with you anything that you really want to have during the next year and a half." At this point the Senior Chaplain realized there had been some lack of communication and asked if I had been informed of this move. On learning this was the first indication I had received of any move, he suggested that I consult my commanding officer, Dr. Warren, and report back to him without delay.

Reporting to the Administration Office, I was informed that the CO was busy, so I requested to see Major Palmer, the second-in-command, and reported, "I seem to have a problem. It appears you chaps are trying to get rid of me, but you haven't told me anything about it." When he expressed surprise and disbelief, I told him of my telephone call. It was the first he had heard of any move for me, so he telephoned the CO, who replied: "Oh, send him over; I've been trying to get him on the phone."

I walked across to the CO's office, where I met the Senior Chaplain from Aldershot, who was most apologetic. He had been delegated to inform me two or three weeks earlier that I was on embarkation standby for a battle zone and was expected to report at Blackdown that afternoon, but had omitted to tell me. Other chaplains, friends of mine, knew of this new development, but it would have constituted a breach of security for them to mention it to me.

The situation finally clarified, I walked back to my office, telephoned London, and explained the situation. I pointed out my difficulties in maintaining secrecy about the move unless I, as Education Officer, visited the wards that afternoon to bring books I promised the men, and to continue my evening meeting. London agreed that, under the circumstances, I had no alternative but to carry through with those plans, but that I must report at Blackdown no later than 0830 hours the following morning. So I spent most of the night readying myself for the move, stuffing everything I had into two packs and my bedroll. I sent my trunk off for storage and next morning duly reported for new duties at Blackdown.

There I spent the best part of a day preparing myself along with others for embarkation to a war zone—obviously Italy. I was to become part of a detail of forty armoured corps officers who were being sent out as reinforcements. All my infantry equipment was taken away and I was issued, among other things, black battle dress, a beret, and a tank helmet for the armoured corps. We had individual pictures taken for our ID cards, received the required inoculations, and started taking mepacrine pills, one a day, in preparation for entering a malaria-infested area. That evening we entrained for Liverpool. On the morning of November 11, 1943, we marched aboard ship and proceeded overnight to Gourock, Scotland, where we joined forty-nine other ships of the convoy. We moved out overnight, accompanied by an armada of corvettes.

Having set sail, the convoy moved due west for five days as though headed for New York. Then, in mid-afternoon one day, whistles blew and lights flashed on our forward starboard side. The corvettes cut through the convoy like a pack of hounds. Each ship, ours being a ten-thousand-ton passenger boat filled to capacity, turned directly about and inside twenty minutes the whole convoy was moving in an easterly direction. The convoy again turned south and, after passing west of the Azores, turned east and approached the Strait of Gibraltar, sailing north along the coast of Africa.

An earlier convoy, including a hospital ship, had been torpedoed in the Mediterranean, but we sailed through without any interruption. Our ship put in at Algiers, where our detail of officers and others was put ashore and transported out to the town of Blida, approximately thirty miles southwest of Algiers. There we camped in tents on a large plain at the foot of the Atlas Mountains and spent three weeks bodybuilding and tramping up into the mountains, readying ourselves for action in Italy.

There I had my first experience of a hurricane. Late one night, after a very hot day, a terrific wind flattened our tents and outbuildings, accompanied by a downpour that soaked everything. After the storm passed, we got up, shook the water off the canvas, put the tent back up and returned inside to our dry bedrolls. We had just got back to sleep when the strange calm that followed the whirlwind was succeeded by another blast, this time from the opposite direction, and our tent went down again in more rain. So we simply shook the water off the canvas and slept as we were until morning. The eerie calm was the eye of the storm as the hurricane passed over us. No one was injured and in the morning we put our camp together and carried on as usual.

After three weeks—by now the latter part of December—we boarded a small British troopship that had been in service in the Indian Ocean. The baker on board made fresh bread and rolls for breakfast, which appeared to be made from a light brown flour. When we broke them open we discovered that the small brown flakes of wheat were actually tiny ants. We were assured that the ants would do us no harm, and were, in fact, another source of protein. The rolls and bread were delicious to taste, and so were devoured by the passengers. We put in at Naples harbour on December 20, and were transported out to Avellino. The next day I boarded a train travelling north. I arrived just before Christmas at No. 4 Canadian Base Reinforcement Depot, the final dispersal point for reinforcements before being sent to fighting regiments where they might find themselves engaged in action against the enemy as soon as they arrived.

No. 4 Base was at that time located at Lucera, a town that has stood from Roman times on an isolated rocky fragment of the Apennines, rising five hundred feet above the surrounding plain. This had been the starting point for the 1st Canadian Division attack in the main drive north. We could hear enemy guns to the north and west across the valley, and the men were nervously aware of the nearness of their own involvement in action. Colonel McRae, commander of No. 4 Base, had requested that I remain with the unit as long as possible. He agreed that I should have an opportunity to speak to each consignment of reinforcements as they arrived and make myself available to any man who wished to see the chaplain. I was kept busy.

It was here that I began to keep a daily journal, to collect data for my monthly reports to the Senior Chaplain and also for the many letters it became necessary to write on behalf of men with particular needs. I decided it would be an account of what I did and experienced each day, to be recorded at the end of each day, if possible. With increasing pressure on my time and attention, I also needed to formulate some simple and practical way of keeping myself in contact with the Christian tradition of faith and life in the face of the surrounding confusions and contradictions. As a basis for meditation, I decided to read one chapter each day from the small King James Version of the New Testament that I carried in my breast pocket. This I did, commencing with chapter 1 of the Gospel according to St. Matthew on New Year's Day, 1944. I recorded at the head of each chapter the date and sometimes the place in which I was situated at the time.

At this point I had my office and living quarters in the office of what had been a livery barn. It was bright, clean, and warm, and I attracted some interesting visitors. On January 6, 1944, the feast of the Epiphany, there appeared a man who introduced himself as Captain Bullock, in charge of War Graves Registrations. He said he did not wish to disturb whatever I was doing but just wished to sit quietly and warm himself. So I made a cup of tea and opened a Christmas cake that my wife, Hope, had made and given to me when I left Brockville in late September 1943. We both enjoyed the cake, a small touch of Canada all the way out there in Italy, and talked together about many things. What he did not tell me was that he had been the commanding officer of the West Nova Scotia Regiment; in fact, he had mobilized the West Novas and led them overseas as part of the first Canadian troop convoy. But because of his age, he was not permitted to lead troops into battle. So the regiment went off to Sicily under new leadership, leaving him behind in England.

Lieutenant Colonel Bullock reverted to the rank of captain to be eligible to be sent out to Italy in charge of War Graves Registrations and to be near his son, Capt. Reginald Bullock, then serving with the West Novas in Italy. Reg was mortally wounded in the battle for Ortona. One of his doctors knew the seriousness of the wounds and summoned Reg's father, who was working in the Ortona battlefields not far away. Lieutenant Colonel Bullock was able to visit Reg in hospital and was present when he died; the next day he assisted in the Church of England burial service. When he called on me he was on his way back down the line.

Reflecting later on this unusual visit, it is evident to me that my Captain Bullock may have had another particular reason for his unexpected call. Captain Brundage, the chaplain of the West Novas, had been invalided out with jaundice during the battle for Ortona and was not expected to return soon to front-line duties. It was known that a reinforcement chaplain was available at No. 4 Base. But what sort of man was he? Would he be able to meet the spiritual needs of the men whom then Lieutenant Colonel Bullock had personally recruited and led into this maelstrom? I did not know at the time that there was a vacancy in a regiment. The West Novas was simply one of the many regiments in the fighting force of 1st Canadian Division, whose reinforcements were passing through No. 4 Base. It was only later, after I had been attached to the West Novas, that I realized the importance of some of the questions Captain Bullock raised during that brief visit. So much was left unsaid.

CHAPTER TWO

Ministry on the Arielli Front
February–March 1944
Casa Berardi / Ortona

O<small>N FEBRUARY</small> 10, 1944, I was struck off strength of No. 4 Base and posted to No. 3 Canadian Infantry Brigade, 1st Canadian Division, for attachment to the West Nova Scotia Regiment as chaplain. I brought with me Pte. W.G. (Bill) Elliott, whom I had trained and who had worked with me in Halifax, as my assistant in the chaplain's office. We were picked up by jeep at headquarters, received directions from the Senior Chaplain, and set out at 1100 hours, to locate 3rd Brigade HQ, which, it turned out, was on the move to a new location and had not yet arrived. Obtaining fresh directions, our driver set out for the West Novas' rear battalion HQ, but took a wrong turn. We spent an hour and a half stuck on a gully hillside north of Ortona while the enemy lobbed shells into a ravine nearby. We had been heading into the enemy lines. We retraced our route, got new directions, and finally arrived at Casa Berardi, the home of B Echelon of the West Novas, where we settled in for the night.

Casa Berardi, a three-storey farmhouse overlooking the road junction of the Orsogna–Ortona highway, was captured and held by Capt. Paul Triquet's company of the Royal 22nd Regiment in the face of persistent and heavy mortar and machine-gun fire and counterattacks by tanks and infantry in the final phase of the battle for Ortona. For his bravery and outstanding leadership Triquet was awarded the Victoria Cross. The old Casa had a number of large holes in its roof from shellfire, but the walls, made of stone, were sound. It was now used as the West Novas' rear battalion HQ, where reinforcements were delivered. The new arrivals, hearing of these heroic battles, gained a deep respect for their officers and brother soldiers.

Officers arriving as reinforcements were billeted in the old Casa and set up camp beds on the top floor. Holes in the roof were covered with a huge tarpaulin that sagged under heavy loads of snow. When the snow melted during a warm spell, water on the floor gave us an additional hazard to cope with. The other ranks lived in slit trenches, each covered by a pup tent to hold off rain and snow, which fell almost daily at this time of year. A Canadian artillery unit was stationed below a hill directly behind the Casa, and I well remember, on my first night, being awakened by their shells passing directly overhead on their way to the enemy lines.

At this time the West Novas were holding a section that became known as the Arielli front. They occupied a deep gully created by the Riccia stream, and the men on duty spent much of that winter living in caves in the walls of the gully, coping with snow, rain, and mud. The ground was not frozen so that even though the snow might be deep, the soldiers' boots sunk into mud with each step. The companies alternated duties, two in the line and two out, throughout the winter of 1944. The men who were off duty occupied ruined houses in the little village of Villa Grande, which had been destroyed by shelling during the battle for Ortona.

The regiment had been without the services of a chaplain for several weeks, so there was much catching up to do. I spent my first day with the regiment doing nearly the same job I had been doing for the past six weeks at No. 4 Base—interviewing men who had problems and speaking with their senior officers in an effort to get them some help. The only difference was that these men had been engaged in the grim business of fighting a war for the past seven months and had all learned of urgent problems at home. Several were seeking compassionate leave to Canada. My responsibilities also included pastoral care and arranging Sunday services for the Carleton and York Regiment and Brigade HQ, their chaplains being off getting some much-needed rest.

The snow and rain continued and it was impossible to plan an open-air service at rear battalion HQ, but I did manage a service for the Carleton and Yorks at San Lorenzo in an oblong room used to billet reinforcements. Their equipment was piled against the walls and we set up a table for an altar and draped it with a flag. Our only lights were the two candles on the altar. A forgotten rifle was left hanging on the wall behind the altar, creating an image that I thought symbolized the paradoxical situation in which we found ourselves. I called the congregation's attention to the two lights on the altar, the one symbolizing Christ, the Light of the World, and the other reminding us that Christ had also said to his disciples, "You are the light of the world," a challenge that was particularly relevant in the confusion of our present situation. On the following Wednesday I held a Padre's Hour with twenty-five men who had just come up for their first taste of battle. Private Eisnor came to see me for help in locating his brother, who was serving with the West Novas. Later in the week I brought

Southern Italy, 10 July 1943–9 June 1944

his brother, Perry Eisnor, down to see him. I also met Private Langley, whom I had known at No. 2 Canadian General Hospital at Bramshott, England.

So ended my first week with the West Novas. I had made contact with many senior people with whom I would be working for the next eighteen months and attended to a number of requests needing immediate attention. However, I was disappointed that I had failed to meet any of the West Novas who were fighting in the forward area or in reserve, occupying houses throughout Villa Grande and the surrounding farm community. It was because I wanted to work with such men that I had volunteered to serve in the Chaplain Service in the first place.

I had yet to meet the commanding officer and was anxious to do so, but the chaplain's truck was in the shop undergoing major repairs. I consulted the quartermaster, who made daily visits to tactical HQ, in the hope of obtaining a ride to meet the CO. He told me the CO declared he did not wish to meet the chaplain at that moment and wished me to remain at rear battalion HQ for now. The CO's dismissive attitude annoyed me. I was not exactly a newcomer to the service, having served for a year with the Black Watch in Canada and on the staff of No. 2 Canadian General Hospital in England and Canada, and I was fairly well acquainted with my responsibilities as a chaplain to a regiment. But I recognized that this was my first contact with a regiment engaged in war, and one that had already experienced seven months of heavy fighting.

The commanding officer, Lt. Col. R.S.E. Waterman, was a professional soldier of the Canadian permanent force and had been second-in-command throughout the campaign until the previous commanding officer, Lt. Col. M.P. Bogert, was seriously wounded in the battle for Ortona. Major Waterman then took command and gave outstanding leadership throughout the remaining ten days of the battle. He had been confirmed in his command and promoted to the rank of lieutenant colonel, with all the problems of adjusting to his new responsibilities and establishing his own pattern of leadership. So I decided to temporize for a few days, make contact with those who were ready to see me, and attend to a number of specific calls requiring immediate attention.

Having spent a week orienting myself to personnel and the general area, I was now ready to move out to make contact with the men in the reserve area around Villa Grande.

Reinforcements were coming in daily to be accommodated overnight in the cluster of slit trenches. When my now functioning truck arrived I had it parked in a prominent spot in the yard with my padre sign up so that anyone who wished might contact me. Beyond this it was impossible to do much more than have a casual word with the men as they moved through the process of being assigned to the companies.

On Thursday, February 17, I decided to make contact with men of the rifle companies in reserve who were billeted in and around Villa Grande, despite the CO's concerns about the possible deleterious effects of a new chaplain visiting his fighting troops. After all, the chaplain's central duty, according to the written instructions, was to strengthen and help maintain the morale of the fighting troops. I wanted to meet these men and learn from them how they were faring under the miserable conditions of an Italian winter.

First I visited the platoons of A Company, billeted in houses scattered along a valley just south of Villa Grande. Here I had a pleasant surprise. As

I entered a small, dark house in which the men were clustered about a fireplace to keep warm, one of them came towards me with his hand out. "I believe," he said, "you are Laurence Wilmot, from Clanwilliam," and I greeted Clinton Wright, whose father ran a barbershop and pool room in Clanwilliam, Manitoba. I had not seen Clinton since my school days when we used to spend Saturday evenings getting our hair cut or playing a friendly game of pool. Later, on a subsequent visit to this platoon, I had Clinton cut my hair for old times' sake to recall more peaceful days.

Later that afternoon, I set out to visit men of other companies close to Villa Grande, but ran into a concentration of shellfire. We took to the ditches while some shells and Moaning Minnies exploded nearby, but they did little damage. The shelling continued in Villa Grande, so we turned about and visited a platoon of A Company billeted in a demolished church. The heavy shelling continued. Everywhere I went the men were glad to see me and I determined I must get out to Villa Grande to visit the others who were billeted in ruined houses throughout the village.

One of the great blessings of having my truck was the provision of a place to be alone with myself and with God. In my civilian ministry I had regularly spent an hour in prayer and meditation on the Scriptures and pondering the day ahead. I determined that, as far as possible, I would continue that practice throughout my ministry with the troops. After such a time of quiet prayer in my truck, I set out on Friday morning for Villa Grande to visit other companies in reserve. I found D Company in town, the platoons well spread out and mostly in strong, dry billets with either a fireplace or a tin stove to keep them warm. What a welcome change from the dark, dank caves in the forward areas! Here, again, I found a ready welcome from the men and their officers and began to feel very much at one with them.

The men spoke of their homes and families and enquired after their new padre. But they quickly focused on the fact they had been without a padre for more than a month, and that some of them had not been able to make their Christmas communion. Here in Villa Grande it was neither permissible nor wise to have a large gathering, but the men would be glad of services in their platoon billets, if this could be arranged. The enemy made a practice of shelling the little village intermittently, and I had to take cover on a number of occasions as I went from one platoon to another visiting the companies. I then walked out to the south edge of town to pay a call on the CO to discuss with him the possibility of holding services with the men in their billets.

This was my first meeting with Lt. Col. Ronnie Waterman, the CO of the regiment, and it gave every promise of being a confrontation. Giving me no time to explain what I had come to request, Ronnie launched into a tirade about chaplains, declaring that he would not lay on a church parade here in the battle area, but that these men were heroes and deserved everything they wanted whenever they were out of the line. He would provide trucks to bring them back to the canteen at Lanciano, or some other place, where they could find every pleasure they wanted, but he would not lay on a church parade. He even stated that he wished the regiment could get along without a chaplain but that, unfortunately, there were times when one was necessary, referring, of course, to the need for someone to conduct a burial service. He advised me to remain at rear battalion HQ unless specifically called forward, adding that, he hoped, this would not become necessary.

When I was finally allowed to respond to his diatribe, I explained that I had no wish for him to lay on a church parade. I also told him that while he was away on leave I had been out visiting the men in the reserve areas and some of them had appealed to me to hold a small service for them in their platoon area. I said that some of them were not even able to make their Christmas communion and, if possible, would like to do so. "Oh well," said the CO, "if that is the case, if the men wish to have a service, they shall have it, but because of the danger from shellfire, it will be important for them to meet only in small numbers at a time." I thanked him for his consideration and asked him to notify the company commanders that I would commence services on Sunday. What I did not tell him was that I had already made tentative arrangements with the company commanders. So my first interview with my new CO ended on a positive note. He had granted my requests on behalf of the men. Nevertheless, I was well aware there were many obstacles to be cleared before I could hope to be accepted as a member of the team.

As my truck was laid up for service I spent Saturday morning fixing the stove in the officers' quarters so that it could be lit without smoking the place out. I also made a small collapsible table that could be used in the truck or outside for writing but was also convenient for use as an altar for Sunday services. I rounded off the morning's activities with interviews with two black Nova Scotia men in the guardroom whom I had met earlier in the week. One had been sentenced to two years incarceration and the other was coming up for court-martial. On my previous visit I had found both men very bitter about the treatment they had received in the Canadian army. On this occasion both recognized that they were at least partly responsible for their troubles, and one of them declared his wish to make a new start in life and knelt with me to pray for forgiveness and for an inner power to start afresh.

That evening, while I was preparing for Sunday services at Villa Grande and writing letters home, the shellfire grew very heavy, going in both directions. A few returning shells came perilously close to the old Casa. At 0500 hours on Sunday some fell very near our building, but fortunately none of the men billeted in the slit trenches were wounded.

My first service of the day at Villa Grande was at 0900 hours in a small chapel at the far end of a ruined church that had somehow escaped the worst of the shelling. I held services in D and C Company areas for sixteen and six attendants, of whom fourteen were communicants. On my way back to the Casa I had a visit with Padre Ernie McQuarrie of the Carleton and Yorks, and discussed clearing a room in the ruined church in Villa Grande as a reading room for the men while out in rest area. That night I had a rare, lovely bath, washed my hair, brilliantined it, cut my nails, and rubbed almond cream on my hands and face. But the bath was not without its difficulties. Every time I made a move to get ready for it, Jerry would throw over a few shells, but I finally decided that if I was going to get hit it wouldn't make much difference either way, and I needed the bath now, so I stepped into it.

So commenced my Christian ministry among the officers and men of the West Novas, a tiny cell in that vast army of men and women engaged in the ordeal of the ages, the outcome of which would determine the future direction of human history. For the next year I was to work with these men as they carried out the grim tasks that destiny had assigned them. Throughout those months I made an attempt to continue the ministry in which I had been engaged for eleven years as an Anglican priest in Manitoba, where people were struggling to survive an economic depression that had robbed most of them of their means of livelihood. There, people were being slowly destroyed through frustration, isolation, and poverty. Here in Italy and elsewhere the sons of those men and women were engaged in the task of destroying an enemy whose avowed aim was the subjugation of mankind to the will of the so-called master race.

What was I doing here? What part could I, a Christian minister, play in such an undertaking?

I had entered the Christian ministry because of my awareness of God as a living presence at work in the world, and because he had disclosed himself and his purpose for my life to me. Preposterous as it seemed to me as a youth, I became convinced that this divine being was calling me to bring to men and women of my generation the message of his great love for all mankind, a love that seeks to bring peace to men and nations in the here and now of their human pilgrimage. How this was to be accomplished was quite beyond my comprehension at the time, for I was the son of a poor farmer, with no financial resources and a mediocre education. But the vision and the inward conviction persisted and became the all-absorbing passion of my young life, resulting in six years of university and college education and my ordination in 1931.

Chapter Two

At thirty-seven years of age, I had adopted patterns of behaviour that formed the context of my ministry. In peacetime I would arise around 0500 hours for prayer and meditation, usually upon some passage of Scripture. For an hour and a half I would ponder the day ahead of me and bring before God the needs of the people and problems of which I had become aware. Following breakfast, I would go into the church for matins, then spend, when possible, an hour or more at some ongoing study designed to enrich and deepen my understanding and preparedness for whatever tasks God might call me to undertake.

Throughout the intervening years it had been my aim as I moved among men and women in rural Manitoba to bring to all, as far as possible, a sense of God's presence, calling men and women into a relationship of personal faith in him and his purposes for their daily living. I was now commencing what seemed to me to be the impossible task of proclaiming the peace of God to men committed to the grim prosecution of total war.

The young men among whom I was now serving routinely faced the possibility of death in combat during nightly fighting patrols in the forward area, or from the shelling of their billets while in reserve. Many of them were no more than eighteen years of age, some even younger. I was familiar with the guidelines issued for the conduct of my various services as a chaplain and responded to their expressed needs in this situation. I realized, however, that the situation was rapidly changing. During these early weeks I lived at Casa Berardi, slept on my army cot in the officers' quarters, had my meals with them, and used my truck as an office and a place for privacy to pray and meditate and for interviewing men while at rear battalion HQ.

In the forward area, while visiting men in and around Villa Grande, there were few opportunities for privacy in their living quarters, and even after the weather warmed it was difficult to find privacy for visiting outside. On one occasion, I brought a lad who had a serious problem that he wished to discuss to the far side of a garden, where we could be alone in what appeared to be a fairly safe location. Here we sat side by side on a piece of turf turned up by a plough. But as we were nicely settled into the interview, something whizzed past the back of my neck and tore up the earth in front of us. We both moved without comment, realizing that someone had us in his sights. Also, as I walked about the village, I learned quite quickly to be alert to an approaching shell and to seek shelter behind walls or a stone fence.

Apart from these occasional reminders, I was in no immediate contact with the enemy as yet, but realized that as spring approached we could expect to be pushing on with the task. In the meantime I was getting to know the officers and men of the regiment by visiting them in their billets whenever possible and on Sundays arranging short services for platoons, mostly in their living quarters, while they were in the reserve area. My daily round usually consisted of early morning prayer and meditation followed by such study as time would allow, and the balance of each morning was usually spent in attending to daily correspondence. The early afternoons I devoted to interviews, usually in the truck, or paying visits to men in reserve in the Villa Grande area.

The pressures on my time were tremendous, and I realized that I could easily be driven by emergencies and lose my way. I determined that at some point in each day I would find time and place to be alone and to read and reflect upon a chapter of the New Testament. I also memorized, and took as the charter of the service in which I was engaged, a passage in Paul's letter to the Ephesians, 6:10–20, which in the New English Bible translation, reads:

> Finally then, find your strength in the Lord, in his mighty power. Put on all the armour that God provides, so that you may be able to stand firm against the devices of the devil. For our fight is not against human foes, but against cosmic powers, against the authorities and potentates of this dark world, against the super-human forces of evil in the heavens. Therefore, take up God's armour; then you will be able to stand your ground when things are at their worst, to complete every task and still to stand. Stand firm, I say. Fasten on the belt of truth; for coat of mail put on integrity; let the shoes on your feet be the gospel of peace, to give you firm footing; and, with all these, take up the great shield of faith, with which you will be able to quench all the flaming arrows of the evil one. Take salvation for helmet; for sword take that which the Spirit gives you—the words that come from God. Give yourselves wholly to prayer and entreaty; pray on every occasion in the power of the Spirit. To this end keep watch and persevere, always interceding for all God's people; and pray for me, that I may be granted the right words when I open my mouth, and may boldly and freely make known his hidden purpose, for which I am an ambassador—in chains. Pray that I may speak of it boldly, as it is my duty to speak.

I felt frustrated in my inability to visit the forward troops during these early weeks with the regiment. During my years in a rural ministry I had made a practice of visiting people where they lived and worked, especially when there were problems. People desiring to be married or to have their children baptized came to see me either at the church or in the rectory. When there were serious problems, though, I went to the source to get a better picture of the total situation than words could convey. Here, however, it was not possible for me to visit the men who were occupying a section of the front on the opposite bank of a steep ravine immediately north of

Villa Grande. They were living in caves and dugouts and sometimes in the few remaining abandoned buildings. Amid alternating rain and snow, and the constant mud, they eked out an existence by day, unable to move out of their dugouts that were under constant enemy observation. At night they held themselves in readiness for patrol duty or to fight off an enemy attack.

The Arielli front in 1944 was in a situation of static warfare similar to that of Vimy Ridge in 1917. Fighting patrols, consisting of a junior officer and ten or so men, went out night after night to make contact with enemy outposts and forward positions. Sometimes they had specific instructions to bring back a prisoner, or simply to shoot up a position that the enemy had attempted to occupy at night as a machine-gun post. In this manner the men and junior officers, many having recently joined the regiment to replace casualties from the battle for Ortona, were "blooded," as the CO called it. Thus they became acquainted at first hand with the grim reality of war, and familiarized themselves with the terrain and the disposition of the enemy directly before them.

The interrogation of captured prisoners also provided valuable information. These patrols kept the enemy on the defensive, which discouraged him from attempting a major infiltration into our lines, but they were costly in human resources. The men spent from ten to twenty days living and working under these conditions, to be followed by five days of rest behind the lines before going in again. The Arielli front, termed a "sit-down" war by some, was anything but that for the men of 3rd Brigade. That winter it cost the West Novas thirty-nine men killed and 124 wounded, including many veterans who had been with the regiment from the beginning. To render my task doubly frustrating, it was difficult even to see the wounded. They were sent out immediately from the forward area to a central casualty collecting post, where an ambulance took them to one of the field dressing stations or to a hospital. I would only learn about this in the morning, by which time it was difficult to locate them. However, I soon developed an information pipeline through officers and men who knew of my concern and was able to see many of the wounded before they were moved further down the line.

By the first of March I was finally making some headway in my attempts to minister to the officers and men in the battlefield. Two days later I packed my truck in readiness to move out to battalion HQ. I went with Quartermaster Whynacht in his jeep to pick out a parking spot for my truck behind a building I planned to set up as a drop-in centre. After visiting with the various sections of HQ and Support Companies—the regimental aid post, the Pioneer and Mortar platoons, and the Sniper Section—I returned to rear battalion HQ for supper, and to fetch my truck. After dark I parked it

Ministry on the Arielli Front 23

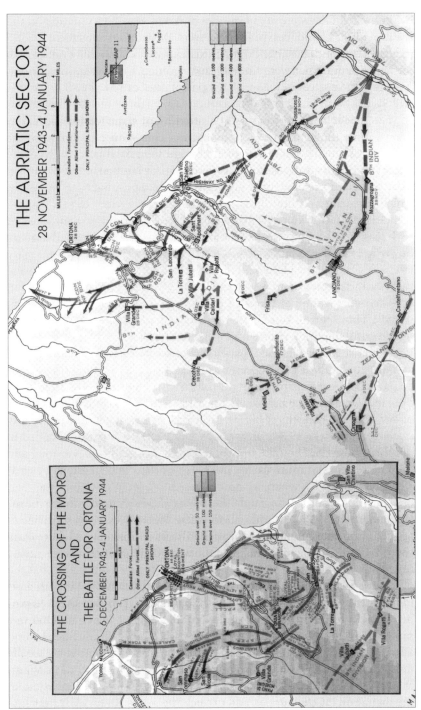

The Adriatic Sector, 28 November 1943–4 January 1944; Inset map: The Crossing of the Moro and the Battle for Ortona, 6 December 1943–4 January 1944

behind the south wall of the house, which was now a meeting place and reading room for the men while out at rest. With this arrangement I could use the truck as an office and a place to sleep while also taking meals with the regimental aid post. I was now in closer contact with the fighting troops.

After all my preparations of the previous day, Sunday, March 5, was dismal. It had rained all night and continued throughout the day. Only seven showed up for a Communion service that I had arranged for HQ Company in the drop-in centre for 0900 hours. A service for C Company was held in a large stone house at the west end of Villa Grande. In the midst of the service the enemy started shelling the area directly in front of the house. All of us simply sang louder than ever to drown out the sound of the shells, which, fortunately, fell short. However, the windows were well sandbagged. That experiment would not be repeated. During the afternoon I visited each platoon of B Company, and in one of them we had a lively discussion on "why men drink too much *vino*." This group all turned up for service later and we had a congregation of about forty officers and men who sang heartily and seemed to enjoy the experience. The fig trees were in blossom and it seemed strange to me as a Canadian to see a tree in blossom before it had leaves. There was still snow on the ground, but in Italy, apparently, fig blossoms are the first sure sign of spring.

A few days later I learned that Lt. W.E. Ingraham, Cpl. Charles Jeremy, and Private McPhee had all been wounded during a night fighting patrol. So on Friday, March 10, I set out for the casualty collecting post, then on to the Field Dressing Station, where I learned that Private McPhee had died of his wounds, Lieutenant Ingraham had been evacuated to the casualty clearing station, and Corporal Jeremy had been operated on. I called in two days later and brought Corporal Jeremy his pay book and mail and found him looking much better, but I also learned that Lieutenant Ingraham had died of his wounds.

During the battle for Ortona the enemy viciously destroyed the beautiful old Catedrale San Tomasso. This cathedral was the reputed shrine of St. Thomas, whose bones were supposed to have been carried there from the Isle of Schio in the Indian Ocean in 1258 and kept in a silver casket under the high altar. While in Ortona I visited this church and met the priest in charge. He was full of guilt because, fearing that the enemy were plotting some dastardly deed to coincide with St. Thomas's Day, December 21, he had removed the little casket and stowed it under the altar in a side chapel. On December 21, the traditional day on which Christians everywhere celebrate the life and ministry of St. Thomas, the enemy totally destroyed the main church building, but the little side chapel was undamaged. The priest was convinced that had he left St. Thomas's bones under the high altar, the cathedral would not have been destroyed. He led me into the chapel, brought out the box containing the silver casket, and opened it. A small piece of wood had broken off the box's fretwork, so he gave it to me, declaring that if I kept it by me throughout the war, I would come to no harm. In deference to him I kept this as a memento of my visit to the shrine of St. Thomas in March 1944.

By mid-March I had a fairly clear picture of the condition of the men of the regiment and their problems. Some of these problems clearly required attention, and without delay. It was time to have a talk with the CO, Col. Ronnie Waterman. His tactical HQ was now in a small shack on the north rim of the Riccia gorge. I accordingly rode out with the quartermaster on his routine evening run. After the quartermaster had finished his business with the CO, he simply reported that the padre had some matters to discuss with him and was waiting in the office. So, having bearded the lion in his den, I was ushered into his inner sanctum. I reported that we must discuss the cases of at least three men who had been away from their families for more than four years. They had all received reports of serious problems at home, but their officers had been unsuccessful in getting them compassionate leave, and I was convinced that something must be done on their behalf without delay. If the prevailing apparent indifference to the welfare of the men continued, it would have a serious affect on the general morale of the troops.

At the mention of needs of the men, the CO was immediately responsive and asked me to write an appeal on behalf of each. He also requested a report on general morale, on what the men were thinking and saying. I saw to it that this report was on his desk the following day! He made no comment after reading it, but requested that I come out with the quartermaster on the next day for an interview. The following evening I was again ushered into the inner sanctum. Ronnie was a superb actor and had a way of speaking that kept you guessing until the final word whether his reaction was positive or negative. On this occasion, as I sat down, there was silence for the space of a few minutes before he spoke. "Padre, I have read your report, and I want to tell you that never in my long army experience have I read a report such as this! I have shown it to the brigadier, and am taking it down to the general at divisional HQ tomorrow morning, and I intend to get action on behalf of these men without delay or my name is not Ronnie Waterman." He then commented on my report on general morale and concluded by requesting that he would like a report on morale each month.

This was a turning point in my relationship with the CO and accordingly with the regiment. From that point on I was invited to attend orders groups held periodically in the CO's office at which all manner of questions were discussed with the senior officers of the regiment. At my first orders group, Ronnie recognized my presence at the meeting by a question that got a hearty laugh from everyone: "Well now, Padre, tell us, how many orphreys do you have on your chasuble?" Everyone, myself included, laughed at this as I had to confess that I did not know what an orphrey was. I did not usually wear a chasuble, but I had done so for a period of seven years while serving as chaplain to a group of English ladies who were engaged in missionary work in northern Manitoba. I would wear a chasuble for their weekly Holy Communion services each Wednesday while serving in Swan River, Manitoba, but it was a plain white linen vestment without any ornaments. I explained that, throughout my ministry in rural parishes, I wore a black cassock, white surplice, and stole at celebrations of the Eucharist and a cassock, surplice, scarf, and academic hood when conducting morning and evening prayer. So commenced a new chapter in my term of service with the officers and men of the West Novas.

While I now had every reason to believe that my services were gradually being recognized as an important component of the functioning of the regiment, I was increasingly being faced with the grim reality of the cost, in wounds and death, of the dreaded nightly patrol. On Friday, March 17, as I was preparing to go to divisional HQ for an interview with the Senior Chaplain, at least four men spoke to me about an admired member of their platoon, Col. Raymond Peach. He had been badly wounded the night before while on a fighting patrol taking machine-gun bullets in the chest and abdomen. They feared he would not survive, but their central concern was that I should see him before it was too late. He was, they said, an atheist, and they could do nothing to make him change his mind.

I called in on Corporal Peach at the field dressing station while in San Vito. He greeted me quietly as I approached his bed. "Padre!! So they sent you to see me!! Tell them for me that they need have no further worry. It has all been a mistake! Tell them He has been here with me all morning conversing with me, and everything is now cleared up. I haven't long left and I am glad you have come. Can you pray with me now?" I assured him I was overjoyed to learn that God had disclosed himself in this way. We prayed together and he shook my hand warmly, if weakly, and asked me, on his behalf, to thank the boys for their friendship and concern, and to say goodbye for him. Needless to say, it was a moment of sorrow and yet of deep joy when I reported on my visit and gave them his parting message. This was, indeed, a memorable experience for me and a great encouragement to his friends. They now realized that their concern for their friend's welfare had achieved what their words had been unable to accomplish. The experience was a further reminder to all of us that God is at work in the midst of us and makes his Presence known in the most unexpected places. Corporal Peach died of his wounds the following morning.

Chapter Three

Taking Up God's Armour
March – May 1944
Casa Grande / Riccia / Montesarchio

By the middle of March it was becoming clear that the miserable Italian winter was behind us and that spring had arrived. Occasional rain had melted the snow, and the sun was warmer and had begun to dry up the mud. Experienced soldiers knew that the tanks would soon be rolling again. But, for the time being, the men had to continue the deadly night patrols.

Having moved out to battalion HQ to live, I now had more direct contact with both officers and men of HQ Company, in particular the medical officer, with whom I could go on the carrier ambulance to visit the companies in reserve. At A Company we heard a lively discussion on an order from higher up to tap all wine barrels and run the *vino* out. The most recently arrived platoon officer was ordered to supervise this task, and it was he who took the blame for spoiling the men's fun. But the *vino* was a real problem. The men were filling their water bottles with the stuff, with serious consequences for those on night watch. So the streets of the little village ran red with wine until washed clean by a rain. The supervising officer was forgiven later when he demonstrated effective leadership ability while leading patrols.

As the mud dried and the roads and trails became firm, route marches were commenced, and I decided to take them as often as possible for much-needed exercise. This gave me the opportunity to meet new men and listen to any problems they had. The march on March 22 was cancelled because of rain. That gave me a chance to read *The Screwtape Letters* by C.S. Lewis, a fascinating account of a wily evil one, Uncle Screwtape, who subtly defeats our best efforts to realize the Kingdom of God on earth. When the rain ceased, I visited around battalion HQ where I had an interesting conversation with Corporal Leaden, from our Intelligence Office, who was seriously contemplating training for the ministry after the war. The

CO, Lt. Col. Ronnie Waterman, took the opportunity of my visit to ask about the morale of the troops. He feared some of the younger officers lacked leadership ability. He also told me that he believed he would be required to lead the regiment into action in a forthcoming spring offensive. I spoke to him about the possibility of Pte. Bill Elliott, my assistant in the padre's office, being posted to a more active role. Bill had enjoyed his few months as my assistant, but clearly felt that he should now join the fighting troops and hoped for a chance for promotion in due time.

That afternoon I discussed the issue of post-war rehabilitation with twenty-five men who appreciated that the government would train them in preparation for civilian life. Another lively discussion ensued on credit unions and co-operative buying and selling, with twenty-seven men attending. I shared with them my personal experience of working with a small isolated congregation in northern Manitoba who were having difficulty in obtaining even small loans from the banks. The banks simply refused loans to farmers during the Depression years. So they formed a credit union, which was most successful. They had only a meagre amount of capital, but they were able to obtain small loans when needed and the money went out and in again three or four times a year, enabling them to survive and gradually build up their assets. This group of soldiers appeared to have done more thinking than those I had visited the day before, where only three out of thirty-five appeared to have any real thoughts and plans for the future. They decided that their next discussion should be on civics and citizenship.

Two platoon officers dropped in for a chat and I promised to visit their platoons for discussion. Lt. Col. Henderson Smith introduced a long discussion on the Christian life, but he really came in to talk about his platoon, particularly about two of his men. I promised to come over the next afternoon for a discussion on rehabilitation with his platoon.

There were frequent conferences of the divisional chaplains throughout the month of March, with discussion focused on three main projects. First, there was a pressing need for a policy on leave to long-service men, especially for compassionate leave to Canada for men whose family situations called for urgent attention. The chaplains took this matter to the divisional commander, Maj. Gen. Chris Vokes, impressing upon him the importance of immediate attention. Second, the chaplains undertook to update the personnel records of those under their care. Each soldier was to be asked to fill out a card providing up-to-date information about himself, his marital status, and addresses of all next-of-kin, in preparation for the forthcoming spring offensive. Third, there was a series of discussions on the government's plans for rehabilitation of the men on their return home. To this end discussions were planned throughout the month of March, to be held with groups of men of platoon strength. Each man was encouraged to complete a questionnaire indicating his vocational preferences.

In the afternoon of Saturday, March 25, I attended a meeting at divisional HQ with General Vokes and my fellow chaplains. The general gave us quite a lecture. These men with low morale, he declared, had volunteered, and should be told to buck up and be men instead of moping over what was happening at home. He also reminded the chaplains that it was their job to build the men's morale, and he implied, if he did not specifically say, that the chaplains had better tackle this aspect of their duties. The army, he declared, could not afford to be sending men home when they were needed at the front. Then he gave the chaplains an opportunity to speak, and the resulting tempest was hardly what he had expected.

As soon as General Vokes sat down, Stewart East, chaplain to the 48th Highlanders, jumped to his full six-foot, six-inch height and declared, "Now, see here, General!" and proceeded to tell him in no uncertain terms that, unless the army showed some evidence of concern and compassion for these men whose families were breaking down, they and their buddies would be asking themselves why they were fighting at all, and morale would become impossible. Other chaplains then told their stories of what was happening in their regiments, adding more fuel to the fire under the general. When he finally had an opportunity to respond, General Vokes, in a very different tone of voice, congratulated the chaplains on the fine job they were doing, assuring them that the Higher Command was very much concerned about the needs of the men and that appropriate action would be taken on their behalf without delay.

As the most recent chaplain to join the division, I had been struggling to find solutions to similar problems in the West Novas, and I felt a clear sense of relief and satisfaction in the response of my fellow chaplains. General Vokes gained a respect for the chaplains and for their work on behalf of the men, which had not been evident in his earlier remarks.

The bloody business of fighting patrols had to continue as long as we were engaged in "static" warfare. In the early evening of March 28, 1944, a platoon occupied an enemy strongpoint called "King Bird," but was driven out later in the evening, along with a supporting platoon. They suffered heavy casualties from mortar fire, including three killed, fourteen wounded, and one missing. I went out to the casualty collecting post to assist, made a return trip to the regimental aid post and to battalion HQ, and assisted later at the casualty collecting post in preparing men for evacuation. After a short sleep I got up early to bury the body of Pte. Murray Tarr, who had been killed in an earlier battle but whose body had just been brought in from the area in front of the Royal 22nd Regiment. At 1000 hours the bodies of Cpl. John Drake and Ptes. Douglas Rhyno and Willis Dearmond, killed during the night raid, were brought in by jeep. We held another burial service at the West Novas' cemetery.

By this time the weather was fine and I could set my table out in the sun to write letters of condolence to the next-of-kin. From the beginning of my service with the West Novas this had become a regular and most important part of my daily work on behalf of the fighting men. Putting myself mentally in the place of those receiving such letters, I realized that they would already have had word of their loved one's death in action, but it would be important to those grieving at home to get word from someone who had been with or near him at the time and could inform them how he had died. Was he alone at the time? Did he suffer? Was he able to send any message? In some cases I relayed what I had heard from those who had been with him at the time, and in others I had personally seen and talked with casualties as they were being evacuated and so could pass on final messages. Each letter had to be carefully thought out and designed to help the grieving person at home to bear their loss.

That same day I wrote a letter to the wife of a soldier who asked me to seek to heal a widening gap in their relationship, which was wearing thin after more than three years absence on the part of the husband. I also wrote to the forward movement officer for copies of Bible reading booklets for distribution, to the *Canadian Churchman*, a monthly Anglican magazine, for copies for our reading room, and to the Council for Social Service for literature on social problems. I then wrote a letter to my wife, and sent Easter cards to family members and friends. My writing session was interrupted when two soldiers came to see me. I made it a point to see anyone who came to my door, even if I had to miss an occasional mess dinner in the process.

On Saturday, April 1, I left for the forward area with the second-in-command, Maj. Frank Hiltz. After visiting with the regimental aid post staff we went on up the gully to A Company, where we chatted with the men in their caves and slit trenches. I had supper with Capt. Bruce Cochrane, following which I talked with the CO about church services the next day and especially for Easter. I found Ronnie quite in favour of a service in the gully, to which men from all forward companies might come, but he was not in favour of holding a memorial service at the West Novas' cemetery. However, he promised to consult the company commanders on the matter, and authorized me to proceed with plans for Easter services with small groups of men in the company areas.

I spent Good Friday visiting the companies and making arrangements for Easter services to commence early in the morning. At C Company I had an interesting visit with a platoon of the Royal Canadian Army Service Corps, which had been attached to the regiment to get front-line experience.

Later I had lunch with Capt. Scotty Allan at B Company, then on to visit the Mortar Platoon and the Princess Louise Dragoon Guards. Corporal Lodwick, a member of the Guards, knew my brother Walter and gave me his address in the Royal Canadian Air Force in England. After arranging Easter services with D Company, I walked back with Capt. J.K. (Dusty) Rhodes, who was on his way out to liase with the Royal Air Force. We called at A Company to plan a service with them and to visit Capt. Bill Thexton. There were two British officers there of the Maretta regiment from India, which at the time was camped in our area getting ready to take over the defence of this front to allow us to move south in preparation for a spring offensive.

On meeting the two British officers, I inquired whether there were any Christians among the Marettas. They replied that, so far as they were aware, their troops were all Hindus, but that certainly some of the British officers attached to them were members of the Church and would be glad to know of times and locations of Easter services, so that they might make their Easter communion. Before leaving, Bill invited us to drink a small toddy of rum to Dusty's health as he left to visit the air force. Dusty and I had supper at battalion HQ and he caught a ride with the quartermaster back to rear battalion.

On Holy Saturday I had yet another interview with a private who felt he must have compassionate leave but, having listened to his story, I considered his situation did not warrant it. I urged him to face up to the difficult life that destiny had handed to him and to seek the solution within himself. This poor fellow was simply another example of the toll that the long winter on the Arielli front had taken on the men's nerves. In the evening I went to battalion HQ to complete arrangements for a service and Major Hiltz invited me to watch an attack on Bourlon with him. It was an enemy strongpoint that they had tried unsuccessfully to capture the day before. A young Indian officer of the Maretta Regiment came along, and the two of us watched the attack from a slit trench. We ended up discussing the future of India, and the Maretta officer expressed scepticism about Prime Minister Churchill's pledge to give India independence as a reward for services during the war.

The attack, unfortunately, was unsuccessful. One man was wounded and I assisted in rendering first aid to him. Another man had been lost in the attack and no one seemed to know if he was dead or alive. It was decided to mount another attack right away in an effort to retrieve the missing man. At this moment Major Hiltz telephoned the CO and obtained permission to take over command of the attack. I felt this was quite unnecessary, because the young officer commanding the company was handling the situation very well and had the confidence of his men. He was obviously concerned for their welfare, including the man who had been lost out near the enemy strongpoint. It quickly became evident that the change in leadership was not welcomed by the men and was, naturally, resented by the company commander. Moreover, Major Hiltz, who had not been hitherto engaged in front-line action, was highly emotional and demanding of the men. He was not sure how to quietly issue orders so that the attack could proceed in an orderly manner.

The sudden change in leadership and the tensions that ensued had a crippling effect on a young French-Canadian officer whom the major ordered to go out on a patrol and retrieve the casualty. The situation was so charged that the young officer's nerves gave way and he informed the major that he was sorry, but he could not take out the patrol. He was immediately put on charge and sent back to tactical HQ to face court martial. At the request of the major, I conducted the young man back to tactical HQ for a summary hearing. The artillery forward observation officer, who was on hand, was asked to take evidence from the officer, while the CO and I waited in the outer office.

Ronnie, who was walking up and down in the little room, obviously had something on his mind. He turned to me suddenly and bluntly accosted me with a most astonishing charge. "Padre! I hear you have been going up and down among the tents of the Maretta Regiment, in clear violation of standing orders, and trying to convert them to Christianity. I tell you, Padre, I shall not have this. We have had the strictest orders that we must not go near their encampment, and here you are, going directly amongst them. I am going down to see the general tomorrow, and I shall have you court-martialed for this."

I listened in astonishment to what he said and was forced to conclude that the CO was indeed serious in his accusations. I replied, "Well, sir, if you must do that, of course, I can do nothing about it. But, if I were you, I would first check the accuracy of the report. I think someone has been pulling your leg, as a bit of a joke." He did not respond to this but evidently took my suggestion, for I heard nothing further about the matter, except at a mess dinner some weeks later. The officers, evidently having heard something about this exchange, drank a toast to "Wilmot of the Indians," to the chagrin of the CO.

The story, as I had half guessed at the time, and learned later, had originated at rear battalion. Dusty, having been toasted at each company HQ as he made his way back to rear battalion, was asked by someone how the padre was making out now that he was working with the men in the forward positions. "Oh, the padre!" said Dusty. "He is going like a prairie fire among the tents of the Indians, preaching the Gospel to them. Another week here and he will have them all converted to Christianity." Someone conveyed this exchange to Ronnie and he either believed it or put on an act in an effort to frighten me.

Once the preliminary hearing for the young French-Canadian officer was over, I was no longer needed. I returned to the regimental aid post for the night at 0200 hours and to my bed in a cave. It was Easter Sunday morning. The medical orderly had my bedroll ready and I crawled in for a much-needed rest. Then, at his suggestion, I turned a flashlight on the earthen ceiling immediately above my bed and discovered a live scorpion hanging from a root by one leg just above my head. The orderly got a jar of alcohol and dropped the beast into it. I was then able to catch a few hours sleep.

The following day I conducted a series of Easter services in various places, including an olive grove, a gully, and on a grassy slope surrounded by trees with pink blossoms. At C Company, the most forward position, the men had been up practically all night and many had been through hell. The service was so close to the enemy positions that we could not sing for fear of attracting fire.

Originally, my intention had been to hold this service in the C Company office, but it was against standing orders to gather more than twenty men in one room because of the danger of shellfire. The service was, accordingly, held in the open air, with orders to the men to scatter if they heard incoming shells or mortars. Fortunately, no shells were fired, the enemy having exhausted their supplies of ammunition during the night.

I walked back to the regimental aid post and rode in the jeep back to rear battalion. But it had started to rain, so that service, which I had planned to hold in the open air, had to be cancelled. I visited the British tank squadron to inform them that the service had been postponed and I remained there until 2030 hours. This had been a day to remember! A total of 270 men had attended Easter services, some of them in the most forward areas. Sometime later I realized that at times during that day I had been walking in plain view of the enemy.

The events of Easter 1944 constituted a watershed in my ministry with the West Nova Scotia Regiment. These men, who were daily being called upon to put their lives on the line in a valiant effort to rid the world of a tyranny that had enslaved all of Europe and threatened to envelop civilization, readily identified their situation with that young Galilean teacher. This Risen Jesus gives himself to his followers in the breaking of the bread, and has promised to be with us all the way throughout life and death and to a life that is stronger than death. The powers of evil in the world seem at times to be all powerful, but they will fail. The day will dawn when they will be no more. God triumphed over death in Christ and in him we can triumph, by the grace of God who is with us throughout our ordeal. The men responded to this message and from that time on saw the chaplain as their friend and helper.

The CO also seemed at last to fully accept me as his padre, and he made a practice of consulting me on those occasions when my work brought me to battalion HQ. During Easter week Ronnie spoke to me of the difficulties of his role during the past winter. He was well aware that the junior officers and the men hated his guts for ordering them out on night patrols, but there was no other way to obtain necessary information about the enemy and their plans. Now, however, he faced a different situation. He was required to lead the regiment into action in the forthcoming spring offensive and must win their full support. He laid on a series of outdoor picture shows, using the south wall of one of the larger white buildings for the screen. This would provide an opportunity to speak to the whole regiment informally from time to time. He also asked for my support in keeping my ears open and to report on morale, especially on reactions to the new image he was seeking to create.

Finally, on April 13, we moved to Appolinare, as the first step in drawing back from the Arielli front, while the Indian Regiment moved in. On that day, as we were about to leave the front, I received three packages of cigarettes from the Swan River Legion in Manitoba, and two parcels from Hope, one of which was her Christmas parcel. Her parcel had been mailed on October 20, 1943, and took approximately six months to reach me. It was really remarkable, though, how the army kept those parcels moving until they reached their destination. At the time that parcel was posted I was serving as a chaplain at No. 2 Canadian General Hospital, so it had had to follow my journey aboard ship to Algeria and then Italy, not to mention my change of regiment. Letters from Hope would arrive in packages of nine or ten, and some were singed on the outside edges as if they had come through a fire. Yet, they got through to their destination.

One day the CO invited me, together with other officers, into his office to meet Colonel French, the commander of the Indian Maretta Regiment, and two senior Indian officers, the Subadar and Jemidar majors. The Subadar was the Indian leader of the troops under the leadership of the English colonel, who would make all decisions that would then be relayed by the Subadar to the troops. The Jemidar was the quartermaster of the regiment. They were two fine-looking men, short and stocky. As an extra entertainment for the officers that evening, Ronnie laid on a spelling match, which went over well.

Our move back from the forward area did not put us out of reach of enemy artillery, and on Sunday morning D Company cookhouse took a direct hit while the men were preparing breakfast. One man was killed and several others were wounded. I immediately went to the casualty collecting post to learn where I might visit them later and returned in time for our service. It was the first time that HQ Company paraded to a church service since I had joined the regiment.

We were on the move again early on Monday and my truck was moved up to the front of the convoy, a welcome recognition of my standing in the regiment. We arrived at our campsite just outside of the village of Riccia in late afternoon. The regiment had camped there prior to its attack on Jelsi. Capt. Cochrane had supper with me and told me some of the details of the tough fight they had in the capture of Jelsi in the fall.

I visited the men in platoon and section areas and had them fill out their personal information cards. These cards were designed to give me all the necessary information for reports and correspondence in the event of casualties. In the process I spoke with some of the men about their troubles. One fine young man, Pte. G.H. Smith, called about a problem for which he needed some moral assistance. He was by conviction a pacifist, but, realizing this was not enough, he had enlisted in the army as a medical orderly and had become a trained stretcher-bearer in order to assist those who were wounded. Experience in earlier battles had convinced him that stretcher-bearers could benefit from guidance by the chaplain on how to be helpful to men who were dying by praying with and for them. I promised to meet with any whom he would like to call together. Unfortunately, he was killed in action during an enemy ambush on the first day of our next action.

On Thursday I went up to Riccia and borrowed a small organ from the local Roman Catholic monastery church to provide music for our open-air Sunday service. After supper I visited D Company. I chatted with the officers of the company and took the opportunity to discuss a Padre's Hour for their men, something that was being introduced throughout the 8th Army. It was a plan for open discussion with men only in platoon or company strength. The chaplain would introduce a topic of interest and encourage the men to speak out and express themselves. The subject could be religious, social, economic, or any other that they might suggest. The padre himself might propose a subject or problem he was concerned about and enlist their assistance in thinking it through. The officers all agreed this could be a way of strengthening morale. I also mentioned my need for a choir for Sunday services and for an organist. Regrettably, the monk from the monastery called on Friday to inform me that the ecclesiastical canons prohibited him from loaning me the organ. After some telephoning, I set out in the afternoon for Campobasso, where I obtained a small portable organ from the Third Line Shops.

Chapter Three

On Friday the CO held a two-hour meeting of all officers of the regiment to inform us of plans for the spring offensive. Ronnie then gave detailed instructions for a scheme in which we would all be involved. Following an early supper, the officers of each company would set out on a cross-country hike under the leadership of their company commander. If anyone failed to complete the hike, he would be left off the team to go into the forthcoming action. All were required to map-read their way through a particularly tricky piece of country that was criss-crossed by innumerable ridges and gullies. If any leader misread the map and took the wrong ridge or gully his group would end up miles from the agreed destination. All went well with HQ Company officers until we entered a series of gullies, at which point Ronnie personally took over control of our group. He misread the map and we had an exhausting experience extricating ourselves from blind gullies. Ronnie was completely exhausted and, in the midst of a long climb up a winding road, was persuaded to accept a ride in a jeep sent for him when we failed to arrive at the arranged rendezvous. Needless to say, he made no further reference to his stipulation about finishing the course. Nevertheless, the officers of each company were required to lead their men through the same exercise, taking off at midnight.

Sunday turned out to be cold and blustery, but the sun came out periodically. I held a voluntary service on the lee side of a hill. Maj. John Cameron read the lesson, Ephesians 6:10–18, in which the apostle Paul exhorts Christians of his day to put on the whole armour of God. I spoke on our struggle and how Paul's message applied to our situation.

The next day I went with Frank Hiltz on a sightseeing tour of Campobasso, where we visited the beautiful cathedral with its Norman colonnades. While I was in meditation in the quiet, Ronnie arrived. The three of us had supper together, after which Ronnie and I returned to the mess with some Princess Patricia officers. One of the officers said to me confidentially, "Do you know that your CO is the most hated and yet the most respected officer in the Canadian army?"

The men hated Ronnie because he had sent them out on night patrols. But shortly after we left the Arielli front, we heard stories that seemed to vindicate his strategy. The British colonel in charge of the Maretta Regiment, which replaced us, decided that because the front was quiet it did not warrant these strenuous exercises. The Marettas sent out no fighting patrols and all remained quiet and peaceful for a few days. Then a 150-man enemy patrol suddenly penetrated a mile and a half through the lines of the Marettas, capturing some important prisoners and documents, and the colonel was enraged. He then sent out a patrol of two stealthy Ghurkas. There was silence until they returned. In the debriefing, the leader reported they had located an outpost where all three guards were asleep. They proceeded to cut off the heads of the men on either side, leaving the man in the centre asleep. On being questioned why they let him live, they said it was important that he should awaken to discover what had happened and report it to his unit. The Maretta Regiment regularly carried out patrols from that time on, but they found no enemy sleeping. Our men came to have more respect for Ronnie after hearing these accounts.

As I rode back to the regiment with Ronnie in his jeep, I told him a little about myself, how I had changed from being an outspoken sceptic to a believer, and had become convinced that God was calling me into the ministry. He, in return, told me about his early years as a boy in England. He had been baptized by Sparrow-Simpson, an outspoken English clergyman whose frequent contributions to the British newspapers I had enjoyed. Sparrow-Simpson had prepared Ronnie for Confirmation, but for some reason, which he did not mention, he had declined to be confirmed. He stated that he now recognized the value of religion and was ready to back me as long as I was doing a good job and helping the men. This was an important commitment for Ronnie, who confessed that when I first arrived at the unit he did not know what to make of me and he did not expect me to last more than a couple of weeks. But now he had obviously changed his mind, for which I was very thankful. It is much easier to do your job when those around you, especially those you work with, know and accept what you are trying to accomplish.

We held a mess dinner at Campobasso, where I met Wallace Rayburn, a war correspondent whom I regularly listened to on the radio, and Colonel Bogert, a former CO of the West Novas who was highly respected by the officers and men. This was our first mess dinner since the winter ordeal along the Arielli front—an opportunity for what Ronnie referred to as an "alcoholic liaison," during which undercurrents of resentment emerged to the surface. I had a long talk with Lieutenant Knowles, who continued to be very angry at the second-in-command for interfering with his leadership of his company in the attacks on Bourlon on the Saturday before Easter. Some of his men lost their lives on that occasion, and he blamed the major for this. That talk with me helped him to unload pent-up feelings of anger. He was a good officer who had built his company into an efficient fighting team. Unfortunately, he lost his life in the Hitler Line battle on May 23.

I attended a joint Infantry/Tank exercise with Ronnie where we were invited aboard a tank for a rather rough ride. I quickly realized why the tank helmet is much closer-fitting than the infantry model. It was fortunate that I had been issued a tank helmet as I prepared for the voyage to Italy, and that I had decided to retain it when I was posted to the infantry.

General Vokes invited me to accompany him in his truck as he assessed the exercise, after which we returned to the regiment for lunch.

The soldiers knew we would soon be moving into action, so those with explicit problems brought them to me in hope of a solution. In the past I had not always been able to oblige, but on this occasion many of the problems concerned pay and allowances for families at home. Our paymaster, Maj. Victor Inman, was particularly good at helping the men with this problem.

On Sunday, May 7, we were on notice to move, so plans for formal services could not be made. However, I held an informal service with B Company in the evening and afterwards a number of men and officers gathered about the organ and we sang hymns until dark. Strangely, as it seemed to me at the time, I experienced little difficulty in playing the hymns on the organ. I had not played the organ for some years, but it all came back to me.

It was Monday before we moved, and in mid-afternoon we arrived at the foot of a high mountain, Montesarchio, just northeast of Naples. I had the personal thrill of driving on a section of the Appian Way down which St. Paul, and later many Christian saints, had trod on their way to Rome, some to their martyrdom. I made my rounds through B Echelon, the Pioneer, Carrier, Mortar, and Anti-tank Platoons, and A Company lines, and listened to a lecture on first aid by our new medical officer, Dr. Hyman I. Mendelson. My assistant throughout the winter months, Pte. G.W. Elliott, and my batman-driver, John, each requested a transfer to more active roles in the regiment. Elliott was to go to the Intelligence Section and John into one of the rifle companies.

Our pause at Montesarchio provided an opportunity for me to visit men in hospitals at Avellino and Caserta, and at the Canadian Convalescent Depot in Salerno. These were important visits because the men there wished to return to the regiment. Several had sent messages to their sergeant or an officer indicating their desire to be back with their friends. It was important that their officers ask for them, otherwise they might be shunted off to another regiment.

By Friday, May 12, the CO had his HQ up and running. It was located in a palatial three-storey house, the ground floor of which he turned into his tactical HQ. He gave a long talk on the forthcoming offensive and the battle for Rome. With great maps and charts on the walls, he instructed us, one company at a time, on the offensive that had already commenced and was going well. This excellent presentation convinced both men and officers that our CO had a clear grasp of the tasks that lay before us and was ensuring that every man knew where he fitted into the picture. General Vokes then came and spoke to the troops, a rather dull presentation after the graphic presentation by Ronnie. He then met the officers in tactical

HQ, shook hands with each of us, and spoke much more directly to us than he had to the men.

By Saturday, there were very good reports on the attack under way north of Cassino. I kept myself busy preparing for a church parade for Sunday and asked Ronnie if he would read the lesson. He agreed, but requested I pick a passage with "plenty of well-rounded vowels." I chose the story of David and Goliath as an appropriate reading for the occasion. That afternoon, after several interviews, I climbed partway up the mountain, away from the swirl of activity, where I spent two hours in prayer and meditation.

At the service on Sunday, May 14, the CO read the lesson, 1 Samuel 17: 38–50, "The Battle Is the Lord's." Ronnie had a true sense of the dramatic. His reading of the story of David and Goliath was a superb performance, and one slight slip of the tongue actually improved the effect. He had been holding orders groups for his officers during the early part of the morning, where he discussed the procedures for calling down artillery fire upon the enemy as needed. When he came to the account of David's encounter with the giant Goliath, he read, "When the Philistine drew nearer to meet David, David ran quickly toward the battle line to meet the Philistine. David put his hand in his bag, took out a stone, slung it, and he stonk him between the eyes; the stone sank into his forehead, and he fell face down on the ground." A ripple of quiet laughter rolled over the troops as they made the connection between the "small smooth stone" that David launched from his sling and the artillery that they were about to call down on the modern-day Goliath. In my short address, I called attention to the monstrous and largely unseen enemy with whom they were confronted and each one of them in himself as little "David." I told the men that as God was unseen and yet directing the battle of Israel against the Philistines, so would he be with them in the forthcoming battle.

Later that morning I held a service for the Mortar Platoon of the Saskatoon Light Infantry, and afterwards went on to visit their machine-gunners. One interview I had that day was very sad. The soldier gave me his home address that I might write on his behalf. He was getting no mail at all, no answers to letters he had written, no gifts of cigarettes, and his children had been placed in an orphanage. He wanted to know why. He was not the only soldier in this situation.

Later, in a call on Ronnie, I was informed I would be travelling with the forward troops but my truck would remain out of battle at B Echelon. I also gave Ronnie a copy of a Bible he had requested. We were on orders to move on two hours notice.

We moved the next morning, a beautiful day. I rode with the regimental aid post in the three-ton truck. Fortunately its tarp was up and protected us from the dust stirred up by the heavy traffic. I spent the journey in quiet prayer and meditation. We camped in a young cork forest of low shrubs that look like oak, below a range of hills. There I visited A and B Company lines and had supper with Capt. Scotty Allan. I found the men to be in excellent spirits in spite of the appalling dust everywhere. They felt ready for battle, which was the reason they came over here in the first place and would remain until the struggle was completed.

After a sleepless night myself, I made my way to C and D Companies where I found them feeling fit after a good night's sleep. I was so glad to be here with the troops going into action, and I prayed for the guiding hand of God to keep me able for the tasks assigned to me. The news of the battle remained very good. Five thousand prisoners had been taken and the offensive was moving faster than expected. We, however, did not move until the following morning.

A Battalion runner

CHAPTER FOUR

Breaking the Hitler Line
May 1944
Pignataro / Pontecorvo

Having slept poorly for most of the night, I got up at 0400 hours on Wednesday, May 17, had a hot breakfast, which set me up for the day, and left for battalion HQ. The regiment had just set off for the attack, and I accompanied them across a field beyond the town of Pignataro, to the Aquino–Pontecorvo road that was to be our starting point. While they waited for the signal to advance, I spoke to those around me and found them in great spirits and ready for the fight. Amidst the din of artillery fire, word came for them to move off, and, because I was visiting No. 16 Platoon of D Company at the time, I set out with them. However, they were moving far to the right of the attacking force, and, well aware that I must remain near tactical HQ, I turned back to locate the CO. By this time he had moved into the field to get a better view of the troops as they advanced to engage the enemy.

My arrival was timely. The Intelligence section of Corporal Leaden and Pte. G.H. Elliott had lagged well behind the CO and he was unable to contact them. When he saw me, Ronnie turned and asked, "I say, Padre, you are a bit of a runner. Would you mind taking a message to Scotty Allan, with B Company at Pignataro, and bring him up to meet me at the crossroads." And so, I became a battalion runner. Pignataro was two miles away, so I was glad that I had kept myself in good physical condition. I found Scotty and his company at a shed on the outskirts of Pignataro and brought them up to the crossroads where Ronnie was waiting.

Just as we arrived, a runner from the forward area arrived to report to the CO that a number of casualties had been collected in a house about 200 yards up the road and around a bend to the right. The MO was urgently needed. However, the regimental aid post had not yet arrived and their vehicles were locked in the convoy, which was proceeding slowly up the road with great difficulty. The intense shelling preceding the attack had blown trees down, blocking the way. Ronnie turned again and asked me to take his jeep and driver and go back, if necessary through the ditches, and fetch the MO and regimental aid post. So off I went and, several hundred yards back, arrived at the head of the long convoy, which had been held up by a large fallen tree. Brig. Paul Bernatchez was supervising the clearance of the road, and when I explained the nature of my mission, he said he had passed the regimental aid post locked in the midst of the long convoy and promised to wait while I went back and brought them forward. So, leapfrogging back several hundred yards more, I located the regimental aid post, brought them forward, and the brigadier led us through the ditches until we arrived at the crossroads without incident. Ronnie immediately became immersed in a conference with Bernatchez, so the MO, Dr. Mendelson, anxious to get to the casualties, asked me to jump in his jeep and direct him up the road ahead. We ran into heavy shelling at the bend in the road and had to take to the ditches again but no one was hit. We soon arrived at a large house where a dozen wounded men had been laid out. The house was forward of tactical HQ for about fifteen minutes, which was really against standard operating procedures for an regimental aid post.

Just as we were completing the evacuation of the most serious cases, an urgent message came from the CO for the doctor to report back immediately at the crossroads. The CO did not want vehicles beyond the crossroads. However, all ended well without casualties to men or vehicles, and we withdrew accordingly. The regiment overran its own objective as well as the one assigned to the Carleton and Yorks, and many prisoners were taken. We thought we had suffered few casualties, until it was discovered that No. 16 Platoon was missing. The mystery of their disappearance was not cleared up for several weeks.

On Thursday, I buried Pte. David Ellement, who had been killed by shellfire the day before. While engaged in this task, I learned of a private in the Royal 22nd Regiment who had been run over by an anti-tank gun and fractured his leg. I located him, splinted his leg, and evacuated him to the casualty collecting post. Later we moved forward and crossed the river on a footbridge while the Engineers built a Bailey bridge for the vehicles. Pte. George H. Lewis was killed here by mortar fire.

I went looking for tactical HQ with Dr. Mendelson but managed to get too far forward, so I sat with two casualties awaiting the jeep ambulance. I carried one of them out when the jeep failed to show up. What happened was that the brigadier had set up his tactical HQ forward of the West Novas tactical HQ. He was in a cluster of buildings that were occupied by the Royal 22nd Regiment tactical HQ, the only habitable buildings between the enemy and ourselves. So the CO of the West Novas, required to be forward of brigade HQ, was compelled to dig slit trenches further forward in

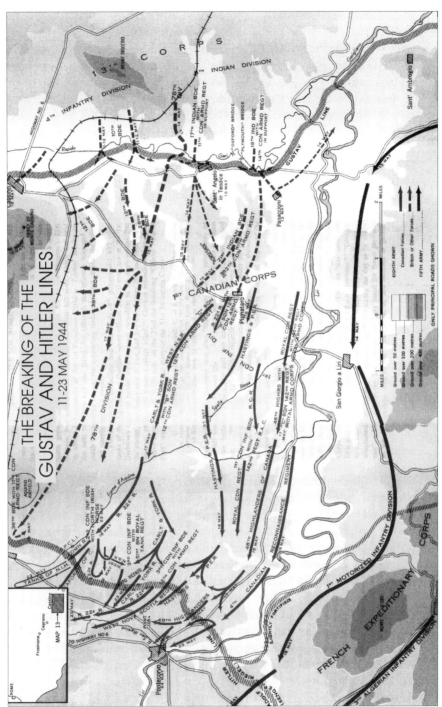

The Breaking of the Gustav and Hitler Lines, 11–23 May 1944

the midst of a grove of poplar trees and within rifle range of the enemy. Plainly it was no place for anyone else except the immediate tactical HQ staff. With bullets whizzing through the trees, Dr. Mendelson and I retraced our steps to the Royal 22nd Regiment's regimental aid post, and spent the night there.

Early the next morning I buried Private Lewis, then returned to battalion HQ for a sleep, completely played out. In early afternoon I went down to the casualty collecting post where I spoke with several casualties on their way out, then went on to the Royal 22nd Regiment to see their casualties, which were very heavy. Next I went forward to our own tactical HQ among the trees, where I buried Captain Rice's batman, a particularly fine young man, and remained for a few hours pondering the inhumanity of war. I returned to battalion HQ and spent the night at the regimental aid post, feeling greatly dejected. The men's needs were so great, and I felt that there was so little I could do to help them. I also greatly missed the time for prayer and reflection that had always sustained me in my peacetime practice. But here, in the field of battle, all I could do was to maintain an openness to God and faith in his presence to guide me under these most harrowing circumstances.

At 0830 hours on Saturday, May 20, it was still raining with no sign of letting up. Word came through that Major Russell, the officer commanding C Company, and several members of his HQ had been wounded by shellfire. I rode out with the carrier as far as possible and walked over to C Company HQ with stretchers, but the wounded had already been evacuated. Among the casualties were three dead. The enemy had pinpointed the position and scored several direct hits, including two on slit trenches, killing those in them, among whom was Major Russell's signaller. The men were badly shaken by such accurate shelling. I set a digging party to work preparing graves, but called it off when shells landed too close to them. We decided to bury the men in already dug slit trenches. It was imperative for the morale of the company that the dead be buried without delay, although it was a risky business because of the shelling. We had to jump into the slit trenches we were using as graves a couple of times to evade mortar fire.

Having completed this sad task, I worked my way back through C Company lines to B Company. While I was chatting with Captain Jones, a Captain Potvin of the Royal 22nd Regiment came crawling through the tall grass from the forward area with wounds in both hands, shoulder, and thigh. He had been reported missing and presumed dead in a skirmish with the enemy the previous night when his regiment occupied this front. I went to C Company for a stretcher and found a man who had lost his nerve and was hysterical. I quieted the man down and brought him out, carrying Captain Potvin back to his regimental aid post. All this activity tired me out, so I returned to battalion HQ, where I sorted the personal effects of the dead and sent them off to brigade HQ. A call came from the casualty collecting post to come and bury a Private Newell of the Carleton and Yorks who had died there, and afterwards I returned to the regimental aid post for the night.

I was awakened at 0200 hours when Private Lambert of B Company was carried in. He had been shot through the chest by one of our own guards as he returned from a listening post in the forward area. The men had become very nervous from the constant shelling and mortaring. I accompanied the chap to the casualty collecting post. Private Lambert seemed somewhat better when I left him, though he was still in considerable pain. I then got about another three hours sleep, but it was apparent that the hectic pace was getting to me. I was discouraged with myself. I could only ask God to take me and do what he could with very poor material for the sake of these men who were enduring so much so bravely. I asked God help me to be worthy of the trust I had been given, that I might be equal to the tasks before me.

On that Sunday morning, May 21, Sergeant Cooper, stretcher-bearer Private Cameron, and Private Manuel of No. 16 Platoon returned, having been absent since the commencement of action on May 17. They reported that ambush and shellfire had wiped out the whole platoon and that Private Kennedy had died of his wounds. I learned from Sergeant Cooper the location of the ambush, so I set out at 1330 hours to locate the bodies of those who were killed. The scene of the ambush was near the little village of Piumarola, far to the right of their objective. It turned out that a British padre had come the day before with a burial party and had removed the bodies. There were rifles and web equipment at the scene of the skirmish, but what had become of the remainder of the platoon was still a mystery.

Early the following morning of Monday, May 22, I buried Pte. Richard Hart of C Company, who had been killed by shellfire. When this sad task was completed word arrived that we were to get ready to move, so I returned to the regimental aid post and hurriedly made a number of wooden crosses for the graves of the men recently buried. These I sent forward to C Company for placement by their members.

Some years after the end of the war I attended a mess dinner at the Winnipeg Grenadiers, whom I was serving as their chaplain. A former tank commander, in addressing the Grenadiers, declared that as he returned from the front in his tank on May 22, 1944, he met four Canadian soldiers making their way up to the forward area, each having a cross strapped to his back. He paused to inquire what they were about and was informed, "This is our padre's idea of efficiency. If we carry our cross with us, then when we are buried the men will be able to mark our graves without unnecessary delay." The officer made no mention of the West Novas or their padre, but, knowing I was the padre referred to, he told the story to get a good laugh, which I enjoyed as much as the others present.

Our move finally took place at suppertime. We moved into a concentration area for the forthcoming attack on the Hitler Line.

That night at the regimental aid post I lay down on a comfortable bed for the first time since I had arrived in Italy—it was eiderdown, with an eiderdown comforter—and I could not sleep. The regiment was going into battle early the next morning, and I was unsure of my role. The chaplain has the distinction of being the sole member of a regiment who is free to do as his conscience dictates during battle; everyone else has to act under orders. Although it was usual for the chaplain to remain at the regimental aid post in order to see all the wounded as they came through, I had spent the past six days of our approach to the Hitler Line interacting between the regimental aid post and the forward areas. What should I do as we moved into a major battle? I needed to pray about the coming day, and so, wrapping myself in the eiderdown comforter, I knelt beside my bed and alternately prayed and slept in that position for several hours. Then, having commended the day and its activities into the hands of God, I climbed into bed and slept until 0430 hours.

The battle for the Hitler Line commenced on Tuesday, May 23, at 0600 hours with the Carleton and Yorks in action for the first phase of the 3rd Brigade attack. The West Novas followed close behind them, ready to pass through when they reached their objective. I was with our men in this first phase. The artillery barrage was terrific and the noise deafening. I detected two men with slight shrapnel wounds, dressed them and sent them back to the MO. When the regimental aid post caught up with me I went on with them to our tactical HQ.

A squadron of British tanks was supporting the battle. The initial phase of the attack led through scattered oak trees and meadowland in which the enemy had hidden Tiger tank turrets mounted on steel-reinforced concrete pillboxes with the guns having a 360-degree traverse. The enemy allowed our tanks to move into the open and then destroyed the whole squadron in a few minutes of heavy shelling. The British major in charge of the tank squadron said the North African campaign was nothing in comparison.

Our regimental aid post shared a room in a large house with the regimental aid post for the Carleton and Yorks, and I decided I would remain there unless some emergency required that I do otherwise. I did not have long to wait. A jeep emerged out of the smoke of the forward area and stopped before our regimental aid post. It was loaded with wounded men from the British tanks. In the front passenger seat was a young tank officer, wounded in the foot, who refused to have his wounds attended to until someone agreed to go and bring in his three men, who, wounded and unable to move, were sheltering in a shell hole beside the burning tank. The tank would soon blow up, and he feared they would be incinerated unless they were fetched without delay. After several unsuccessful attempts, I finally got together a carrying party of six men and three stretchers and went out.

Shrapnel and machine-gun bullets ripped the hazy, smoke-filled air as we set out. To make matters worse, the directions we were given were not very clear. We then encountered a situation with which Canadian soldiers would soon became familiar. As the enemy withdrew, they left behind snipers, hidden in the lush foliage of the oak trees, who took shots at us as we moved along. One of the young men with me was quite concerned and asked, "Padre, what is that hissing noise in the air around us? Those aren't bullets, are they?" I said I was afraid they were, but if we kept moving they likely would not hit us. We were soon out of the sniper's range and sight. Presently I noticed a column of men moving towards the rear and waving a Red Cross flag. Hoping that it was the three we were seeking, I hastened over only to discover a column of German prisoners, one being a stretcher-bearer. I requisitioned the flag and set out once more on our search.

Quite by chance, we came across one of our men from tactical HQ lying in the grass, wounded by shellfire. I dressed his wounds, placed him on a stretcher, and sent him in. With only two stretchers and two bearers, we set out again. We had not gone far when we came across two men lying in a furrow and needing attention. Just as I finished dressing their wounds, a column of prisoners came along. I requisitioned them as bearers and sent them back with the request that the stretchers and more carrying parties be sent up to us. I went on alone and soon found the three men I was seeking, huddled in a shell hole. One had suffered a broken arm, another a broken leg, and the third had lost a lot of blood and was broken up internally. All three were suffering from shock. I dressed the wounds of the most serious case as carefully as possible, but I could not bring him much relief. He was hunched over in the jagged shell hole, cloaked in his army greatcoat. I built up supports with mud and clay to give such comfort as was possible. His suffering from his internal injuries was so terrible that his crew members instructed me to administer morphine from his first-aid kit, after which he dozed.

While dressing and splinting the other two, a pair of walking wounded from a tank crew arrived with minor injuries and burns, so I dressed their wounds too. Together we improvised a stretcher from a door we broke off a German dugout. The slight movement in transferring the most seriously wounded man onto the stretcher seemed to be more than he could bear, and he died before we got any distance. The major fear of the other two wounded chaps was that the fuel tanks in the tank, not more than six feet away, would blow up from the fire that was now a blazing inferno. If that happened they could be covered with flaming debris. Fortunately, when the explosion came, it blew out the other way and did not affect us.

The requested stretchers and bearers failed to arrive. Because the man with the broken arm could walk, I sent him along with one of the new arrivals who knew the way back. With the help of the other new arrival—his hands were burned, yet he worked with his bandaged hands as though there was nothing wrong with them—I managed to lift the man with the broken leg from the shell hole. We carried him to a sunken road, which gave some protection from bursting shells, and laid him behind a large tree. We propped a large door from a German pillbox against the tree to give the lad some protection from the heavy rain that was now falling and assured him we would soon be back with a stretcher. The man with the burned hands needed attention, so I led him to the regimental aid post. There I arranged for a carrying party and went back to retrieve the man we had left under the door. We carried him nearly a mile to the MO, who attended to him and sent him on to a field hospital.

Padre McQuarrie, busy attending to everyone's needs, passed me a cup of tea and a slice of bread and jam. I had barely finished my tea when the CO called us from tactical HQ to send up the carrier for two stretcher cases immediately. But the carrier ambulance was away on a mission to one of the companies, and there was no other vehicle available, so I organized a carrying party with two stretchers and we went up to carry them out. One was a straight case of bad wounds and loss of blood, so I did what I could to stop the bleeding and sent the wounded man off to the regimental aid post. The second was more difficult. This casualty had badly broken legs and a wounded thigh. Using his rifle and a root that I tore from the ground in a shell hole, I made splints and bound his legs together, including a firm bandage around the thigh. We then raised him onto the stretcher and set out for the regimental aid post.

I had been working with carrying parties since early morning, bringing casualties in from the forward area. The whole operation was stalled until the arrival of tanks from the Three Rivers Regiment to replace the British squadron that had been knocked out at the beginning of the battle. I had worked out a pattern of movement that up to this point had proven successful. The enemy were shelling the main road systematically, hoping to disrupt the convoys of supplies that always follow close behind a rapidly moving battle, but the convoys had also been halted pending the arrival of the replacement tanks. So the enemy shells were falling approximately fifty yards apart on an empty road. Using a trail about fifty yards to the right of the main road, the parties of stretcher-bearers could move along parallel to the main road until opposite the regimental aid post. There they would wait until a shell had landed and then dash across. On this occasion, as on others, I proceeded to lead my carrying party across the main road, but just as we reached it the enemy dropped another shell.

There was very little warning if you happened to be on the receiving end of those shells, which were either 88 or 105 mm. I was directly in the path of that shell and had no time to make a move even if I had wished to. I didn't move because directly behind me was the carrying party, bearing a wounded man shoulder high on a stretcher. So I simply froze. The incoming shell emitted a terrible howl, which I thought was the music of the spheres for me. It was followed by a tremendous explosion that covered us with dust and smoke. I felt as though I had been hit on the head by a sledgehammer. The blow forced me to my knees. As I struggled to right myself, I called to the men behind me, "Are you all right?" while simultaneously feeling my head for wounds. Blood was spurting out the right side of my head and dripping from the inside of the helmet onto my shoulder and splashing onto my face. The men replied, "We're okay, but what about you, Padre?" Realizing that if there was a hole in my head big enough for me to feel with my fingers I would not still be standing, I said, "Okay, but let's get out of here before they send another one," and led the way across the road and into the regimental aid post without further incident.

I later figured out that a piece of shrapnel penetrated my helmet just above the left temple, was deflected upwards by the tough steel of my tank helmet, cut the cord of the harness that fits it to the head, clipped off a handful of my hair, and passed out the upper right side of the helmet in two parts. Somehow, a small piece of metal, probably from the helmet, came down and nicked the top of my right ear, which was the source of the bleeding. I was deaf and had a severe ringing in my ears for some time afterwards.

I thought I had done a particularly good job at splinting our casualty's legs and thigh and was hoping for at least a little appreciation from Dr. Mendelson, a perceptive MO, but he simply remarked, "He's all right to wait for a few moments while we look at you. Whatever happened here?" After he washed me up, all I needed was a bandage on my right ear. Having fixed up the wound, the doctor asked, "Now, Padre, do you wish me to record this as a wound?"—it truly was a wound, having drawn blood— but I replied, "No, Doc, I think not. I'm all right and there is no point in causing more anxiety for the family at home than they already have." And that was that. But I was feeling pretty shaken up and in need of a short rest. When the MO had attended to the wounded man and sent him off to the field dressing station, he turned to me and said, "Now that I fixed you up,

Padre, I need your help. The tanks have arrived and the Carleton and Yorks have taken their objective. Our fellows are already in action, so I must find a more forward place for the regimental aid post. You've been up there, so perhaps you can help me locate a suitable building further forward."

We set off in the carrier ambulance and, approximately a thousand yards forward, located a large house that seemed ideal for our needs. But, by now familiar with Italian houses, I suggested we test the structure. Taking a small, jagged piece of rock, I tapped the inside wall just above the floor and discovered that the plaster was made from sand and disintegrated at a mere tap. We both agreed this would not do and continued our search. We had not gone fifty yards when the house took a direct hit from a shell and simply disappeared in a cloud of dust and rubble.

A one-storey bungalow several hundred yards further forward could be used in an emergency, but it had already taken a direct hit on one end and there was a dead cow inside. However, in one room there were two wounded men who had been carried there by their buddies, pending the arrival of a carrying party. The MO set to work and had one man splinted and out on a stretcher in short order, but while he was working on the second man the building took a direct hit, fortunately over another room. This building had been made of lime and we were all covered with a cloud of dust. Neither the MO nor his patient were injured, but Dr. Mendelson, a dark and swarthy man, came out looking like a ghost. We delayed no further. We loaded both casualties on the carrier ambulance and set off for the regimental aid post. One of the company commanders had located a large house in the forward area that offered the kind of protection we needed, so we moved forward without delay. We had had three close calls within a period of a couple of hours. Was this pure chance? I was too busy to ask the question at the time, but reflecting upon the events of that day, I now believe we were under observation by the enemy and each hit was a direct attempt to destroy us.

The regiment did an impressive job. The long wait of more than six hours for the Three Rivers tanks to arrive seemed to have fuelled them with excess energy. Even when the tanks proved unable to manoeuvre the mud-soaked gully and got bogged down, they pushed forward in a fiercely fought battle that completely overwhelmed the enemy. They arrived at their objective, one of the main access roads to Pontecorvo, at dusk, and commenced digging in, for their orders were that they were to hold on, no matter what the cost. The enemy, meanwhile, were mounting a series of counterattacks. In one of these, German troops crawled up through a wheat field and caught two platoons of A Company unaware. They took about twenty prisoners and, apparently thinking that this was the sole remaining pocket of Allied forces, marched them directly through B Company, who were securely dug in. A pitched battle ensued and the prisoners were released to return to their company. There was sporadic fighting throughout the night, but the West Novas held their ground and were the first regiment of the 1st Canadian Division to break through the Hitler Line.

Throughout the late afternoon and night the wounded continued to come in, so we did not get much sleep. The next day, Wednesday, May 24, was busier than usual. We scarcely had time to organize our new regimental aid post location closer to the newly established front when an urgent call came in from D Company. They had overshot their objective the day before, descended into a field a thousand yards or more west of the road, and occupied a large farmhouse. Enemy tanks gave attack, but Dusty Rhodes successfully called down artillery fire upon them and the tanks withdrew, leaving him and his company secure in the stone building. D Company had suffered a number of casualties with eight seriously wounded men, some of whom had lain exposed to the wet for part of the night. They had to be retrieved as soon as possible. Would the padre organize a carrying party and bring them in? I obtained eight German prisoners of war with a guard from brigade and recruited four of our own men for a party of twelve, with eight stretchers and the carrier ambulance.

We set out immediately to locate D Company but came upon a deep, muddy gully that the ambulance carrier was unable to negotiate. Packing the stretchers on our backs, we set off on a long and rough tramp to locate the farmhouse. The eight casualties had been placed in two rooms and their wounds dressed by company stretcher-bearers. One of the stretcher-bearers had been wounded in the leg by a sniper while retrieving a casualty, despite the fact that he was clearly identified by a Red Cross band on his left arm, as stipulated by the Geneva Convention. The three most serious cases were sent back immediately with the carrying parties I had brought with me. I then recruited three more carrying parties of twelve men from D Company and we set out for the regimental aid post, promising to return with stretchers for the two who remained.

I realized that I should be at the carrier ambulance to supervise and assist the loading of casualties onto the ambulance, so I hurried ahead only to discover I had taken a different route. I turned back to take the other trail when suddenly there was rifle or machine-gun fire and our second carrying party, with their three casualties, went to ground. At first I thought the enemy were counterattacking, but, realizing it was merely a sniper, I started to return. Just then a burst of bullets whizzed past my head and I got down. At this point, I said some silent prayers, as I had frequently done during times of battle. "God," I beseeched, "if you wish us to get these fellows to safety, tell the young man to hold his fire." At that moment an idea flashed in my head. I removed the small Red Cross armband from my left arm and pinned it to the stiff, dry stem of a weed. Waving it like a flag, I got up and returned to the carrying party that had gone to ground.

When the men saw me walking towards them and no one firing, they got up, lifted the casualties from the middle of the road, and followed me. I led them directly past the spot where the firing had come from, waving my flag all the way. No shots were fired. As we entered the relative safety of a stone enclosure we were met by Lt. C. Henderson Smith, who was there with a platoon of Support Company on guard against a possible counter-attack. He said to me, "Padre, how in the world did you come through here without getting shot up? Only five minutes ago I had a man shot and killed who went out to bury a comrade, and yet you walk right through with your carrying parties without a shot being fired."

The enemy shelled us intermittently, and one shell landed on some reinforcements going up to the Royal 22nd Regiment, killing one officer and wounding another. I went over to see if I could render any assistance, but their stretcher-bearers had the situation in hand, so I returned to the carrier ambulance. The road was wet and slippery and the ambulance could not climb the hill, so the casualties were unloaded again and carried to the regimental aid post without any further mishap. It was well after noon by the time we reached the regimental aid post, so after a hurried bite to eat I set out again with two stretchers and carrying parties to bring in the remaining two casualties from D Company.

We took a slightly different route and were not troubled by the sniper, but I brought my Red Cross flag just in case. This second trip was also not without its moments of excitement. Having started the carrying parties on their way back, I remained for a few minutes to converse with Dusty Rhodes about problems one or two of his men had mentioned, and then set out. I had hoped to catch up with the carrying party and assist it at the gully, but before I had gone more than a couple of hundred yards, I was bombarded with Moaning Minnies. I hugged the ground, making myself as small as possible, and waited while the horrible things whined down and burst all about me, tearing up the undergrowth. Fortunately, I was unharmed. The regimental aid post building again proved unsafe so we moved to a larger, more strongly built house, where we spent the night. The CO promised me a large burial party of a hundred men for the next day to gather up our dead and bury them in a marked plot of ground.

Early the next morning I made plans for the burial of our dead with the assistance of twenty men and one officer from each of the rifle companies. We picked a suitable area beside the main Pontecorvo–Aquino road, before a small Italian shrine, which Cpl. Gilbert Rafuse of the Pioneer section staked off, and the men began to dig. Suddenly, a runner arrived with an urgent message to cancel the burial party, return to our companies, and be ready to move in half an hour. We got ready as usual, but the move was postponed until 1400 hours. With the assistance of one or two available men, I located a number of bodies nearby, wrapped them in blankets in preparation for burial, and took their personal effects. Among them was Charlie Lafleche, driver for Quartermaster Cecil Whynacht, who was killed by a shell that demolished his jeep.

At 1400 hours the convoy moved off. We proceeded slowly through Pontecorvo, now reduced to rubble, to a new site opposite a ford on the Melfa River just above the point at which it links up with the Liri. Here we set up our regimental aid post, once again sharing a house with the Carleton and Yorks. The CO ordered me to remain at the regimental aid post during the battle for the Melfa River. This was a great relief, for I realized I had become much too involved in the evacuation of casualties during the past few days. But I was certainly kept busy. The mortar fire was heavy and the river crossing, carried out in broad daylight in plain view of the enemy, brought down heavy artillery fire on our troops.

At one point a tank brought in the sergeant of an anti-tank gun crew who had been wounded. Two of his gun crew had also been wounded and a fourth member killed. I sent stretcher-bearers to attend to these men and the tank picked them up and brought them in, which was much quicker and less dangerous than slowly carrying them a long distance on foot. One of the Pioneers urgently needed help, so we sent the Bren carrier out and brought him in without delay.

In my new role as an assistant around the regimental aid post I learned much by watching. I soon determined that greater organization was needed for evacuating the wounded from battlefield. This was the most evident weakness in the regiment's procedures for a rapidly moving battle. I thought it was essential that those in command realize there were going to be casualties and make provision for their removal to the regimental aid post without delay, and I made it my business to fill this procedural vacuum.

Early in the morning of Friday, May 26, the battalion crossed the river and the regimental aid post moved over with HQ Company. I remained behind with my fellow chaplain, Ernie McQuarrie, and together we plotted out a cemetery and gathered and buried our dead. We had lost two men, Sgt. William Joudrey and Private Williams. The Carleton and Yorks had lost four and a carrier driver from the Royal Canadian Horse Artillery, making a total of seven. The past ten days of intense fighting had been costly in human resources; the regiment had lost fifty-one killed in action, 170 were wounded, and twenty missing. We were put into reserve to be moved south for a much-needed rest and refitting. Before our departure, however, I wrote down, for the CO's consideration, my thoughts on the need for a plan to handle casualties during future action.

Chapter Four

Evacuation of Casualties from Battlefield in Infantry/Tank Operations

Experience in the battle for the Adolf Hitler Line would tend to show there are likely to be casualties early in the engagement among the Infantry moving beside the tanks and, also, that a number of tanks will be knocked out and their crews will need immediate attention. There is urgent need to evacuate the wounded during the course of the battle to overcome the great possibility that they may be run over by tanks milling about. In light of these facts, it would seem imperative that, in such operations, provision should be made for a clearly marked Red Cross scout car or tracked vehicle to follow the battle at a close distance, and to be on call from tanks and infantry to pick up and evacuate the wounded. There is nothing that would do more good for the morale of the fighting troops than some such provision for dealing with casualties on the spot.

Later, when discussing this recommendation with the CO, I raised another matter that I considered to be of even greater concern. We had lost too many of our stretcher-bearers who, despite the fact that they wore the required Red Cross band on their left arms, were being fired upon indiscriminately when attending to the wounded. I requested the CO to take this matter up with higher authorities and ask permission for stretcher-bearers to carry a small Red Cross flag when going out to care for the wounded. My request was turned down by the generals as unnecessary.

Nevertheless, I instructed Corporal Thwaites, the regimental aid post orderly, to take one of his large white bandages, make nine white squares, and sew a large red cross on each. Safety pins in each of two corners would aid in attaching it to a makeshift staff. Each stretcher-bearer and I would carry one of these in his thigh pocket. The enemy could see these much more readily and would be more likely to hold their fire.

Captain George Hooper, Roman Catholic padre from brigade HQ, visited me on Saturday morning and I provided him with a list of the names of Roman Catholic men killed during the spring offensive. That afternoon I returned to the site of the Hitler Line battle with a burial party and faced the gruesome task of gathering up all our dead who had been buried in slit trenches and shallow graves in the company areas. We buried them in the plot we had laid out days earlier before the little Italian shrine.

This was an experience none of us involved would ever forget. Decomposition had already begun, and some of the bodies had actually been disturbed in their shallow graves by scavengers looking for a pair of boots or other loot, prompting some most unkind words about the people of the land. It took weeks to get rid of the smell of death that seemed to cling to us long after the experience. The task continued well into the evening and we did not get back until 2300 hours, tired and hungry. I was cheered to find that four letters and a parcel of food had arrived from Hope.

The next day, Sunday, May 28, I took services for the Saskatoon Light Infantry and the West Novas, at both of which I spoke on the themes of thanksgiving and rededication to the task before us. Later I had a cold-water bath in a brook, my first in weeks.

Relaxation escaped me during this supposed rest period. I needed to write reports and letters to next-of-kin. Writing to the loved ones of those who had lost their lives during the two-week period of our spring offensive was an ordeal. I found it a strain even to push the pen across the page. It was then I realized how exhausted I truly was.

On Monday, May 29, I accompanied Corporal Rafuse and a section of workers to the Hitler Line to complete the work on the graves in the cemetery beside the shrine. It was a sobering experience to go over the battlefield. The area was quiet now and many of the disabled tanks had been removed for repair, but everywhere were signs of the desolation of war. One of the pillboxes, with the Tiger tank gun that had annihilated a squadron of British tanks at the commencement of the battle, remained a silent witness to the grim destruction of war. Its turret had been hit by a British tank, and the explosion of the ammunition supplies had thrown it into the air; it had come down and jammed diagonally across the cement pillbox. Now its long 75 mm gun barrel pointed up to the skies. This military scene became a subject for more than one war artist.

The next morning was nearly a repeat of the day before. I completed more burial returns and continued writing letters to next-of-kin. My rest would have to wait awhile yet.

By the afternoon of Wednesday, May 31, we were finally on the move south to the Piedimonte d'Alife valley to regroup and rest. It was a very dusty and tiring ride. I spent the evening visiting with B and D Companies, where we discussed a subject introduced by one of the men, "The purpose of God in a man's life and the possibility of death"—a pertinent theme for men who had just come out of the chaos of battle in which they needed to kill or be killed. The discussion opened with the suggestion that we had each committed ourselves to deliver humanity from the Nazi scourge, and had put our lives and immediate destinies into the hands of those who were directing the war effort. We were there to do a job, and in the doing of it might lose our lives. Yet, if that occurred, it did not mean that God was not present and at work in that part of his world. As Paul puts it, Christ continues "to save to the uttermost all those who come to God through Him."

I offered my position that we each have a part to play, a job to do, as our part in this tremendous effort to throw back the forces of evil. And although it is man who makes war and only man who can make peace, this does not mean that God was not at work in his world. The evil forces in the ascendancy in Europe and other parts of the world would be defeated by the sacrifice of the lives of a whole generation of young men and women dedicated to the cause of truth, justice, and freedom. This God is with us, and he would ultimately lead us to victory and the opportunity to build a better world for our children.

If we had to give our lives in this ordeal, then that was our destiny, to have lived in this particular generation, and to have had the privilege of dying to open the doors to a better world. All those men whom we buried in the Hitler Line and elsewhere played their part in making this world a better place in which our children might grow up in peace and live out their lives. God is merciful, and those men had gone to be with God. But God is with each one of us every moment of our lives, and if we respond to him, learn about him, and seek to do his will for us each day, he will guide each one of us in our daily thoughts and actions, and we will find a better life here and now and in whatever future there may be for us, as we moved towards the climax of our present ordeal.

At the conclusion of our discussion, Capt. Harry Eisenhauer asked for a burial service to assist him in prayers should it become necessary for him as officer in charge of his men to conduct a burial.

top left, Lt. Col. R.S.E. (Ronnie) Waterman; top right, a Bren gunner at the Hitler Line; middle left, Lt. Col. Frank Hiltz; middle right, Padre Wilmot with Medical Officer Dr. Hyman Mendelson; bottom, three chaplains examine the steel helmet worn by Padre Wilmot during the battle of the Hitler Line.

CHAPTER FIVE

A Tourist in Wartime

June – July 1944

Piedimonte d'Alife / Naples / Rome

The first day of June 1944, a Thursday, we were supposed to move on, but when the move was cancelled I devoted my attention to various other duties. On Friday I went down to the Dental Service at divisional HQ because a wisdom tooth was causing me considerable pain. Imagine my astonishment when the dental officer, who remained in his inner sanctum, told his receptionist that he "was too busy attending to the needs of these glorious lads who have been risking their lives for the rest of us to attend to the needs of a chaplain who, after all, could come in any time to have his needs attended to." I went away shaking my head and thinking uncivil thoughts. Ten days later I had the wisdom tooth removed by another dentist.

That evening my daily reading from the New Testament got me back on track. The reading in question was Paul's second letter to the Corinthians, chapter five, in which he reminds his readers of their new life in Christ and challenges them to make an adequate response. Having pondered Paul's message, I wrote in my diary that mankind's greatest need was reconciliation to God in Christ and then between friend and foe. Only through reconciliation could there be inner peace and peaceful relations between all people.

Early on Sunday, June 4, we learned that United States troops under General Mark Clark had entered Rome instead of keeping up the pressure on the retreating German army, as had been arranged prior to the attack on the Hitler Line. Although he had an excellent opportunity to cut off many of the retreating enemy troops, General Clark apparently preferred to bask in the glory of his victorious army's march through the Eternal City.

On Monday morning I rose early to begin several days of visits to military hospitals. At breakfast the next morning, June 6, we learned from the

German radio that airborne troops had landed in France. This massive airdrop of American, British, and Canadian troops behind the Normandy beaches was the beginning of the D-Day invasion. On Thursday, June 8, I visited a convalescent camp in Salerno to make contact with some wounded West Novas who were anxious to return to the regiment. When staff learned that I was from the West Novas, they reported that one of their patients was a private from the regiment who claimed to be underage and wanted to go home. They wondered if I had any information about him.

I particularly wished to see this young man, Pte. "Red" McAnley, myself, for I had received a letter from his parents stating that he had just celebrated his seventeenth birthday and requesting he be sent home. I met with McAnley and we had a long conversation. I learned he had joined the army when he was just twelve years of age and had gone overseas with the regiment in December 1939. It eventually came out that he was an oversized child, and he was sent home to be discharged and return to school. But school was much too boring for Red and he succeeded in joining up again in 1942. Again he was posted overseas and he rejoined the regiment in Italy on April 19, 1944.

McAuley was one of the few surviving members of No. 16 Platoon, D Company, which had disappeared during the battalion attack on May 17, and through him I learned what had happened to No. 16 Platoon. They had been assigned the right flank in the West Novas attack and soon came under enemy fire, which they quickly silenced. However, in the process, they strayed to the right, deep into the British sector, whose troops were delayed in the attack. Private McAuley was in No. 1 Section, a few yards behind and to the left of the rest of the platoon. When the enemy saw Allied troops approaching, they jumped up out of their trench pits with their hands up in an act of surrender. Seeing this, Lieutenant Langille called his men forward, at which time the enemy fired machine guns from the left and the platoon scattered for cover. The platoon knocked out the machine-gun nest, but a number of men were wounded. The platoon commander, realizing he was out of touch with his company, called to McAuley to take a message to the tanks to come and assist. However, McAuley was wounded before he could complete his task and the whole platoon was taken as prisoners.

Three members of the platoon were killed. The German stretcher-bearers bound up McAuley's wounds and, as the British were attacking, placed him behind a large tree so the Brits would find him, gave him a sandwich, and left. When the British came, they put McAuley in a jeep with some other wounded and sent them back to the ambulance park. Just as they arrived there, they were bombed by the German air force and the jeep was blown up. McAuley landed in a field, relatively unhurt, and was picked up again and taken to a field hospital for attention. That was the end of Red McAuley's war. Having survived that experience he was more than ready to be discharged home as too young for active combat, and I wrote a recommendation to that effect.

The next day set out for Caserta, where I visited Maj. Scotty Allan in hospital and gave him his kit, which had been left behind when he was evacuated. In early evening I returned to the regiment, which had moved since I left.

On Saturday morning General Vokes reviewed the troops and congratulated the regiment on the excellent job they had done in the Hitler Line battle. The CO then brought him into the mess to meet with the company commanders, the medical officer, the paymaster, and the padre. The general asked to see my tank helmet as the Colonel elaborated on my encounter with shrapnel, so I had it fetched. They both had a good look at it. Maj. Bill Thexton suggested I take the lining out to make a loving cup, and give each member of the mess a drink up to the level of the holes. But Brigadier Bernatchez responded, "Don't you do that, Padre. You hang onto that. It's the best souvenir of the war you'll ever get." This I have done, and for years it hung from the ceiling in my study, holding a pot of flowers. I recently donated it, along with an armband and the Red Cross flag I carried in the Gothic Line, to an exhibit in the Canadian War Museum in Ottawa.

Our summer in the beautiful Piedimonte d'Alife valley brought many surprises. I spent one afternoon working with a group of junior officers cleaning up and levelling the earthen floor of the ruins of an ancient stone chapel on our campgrounds. Doors, windows, frames, and roof were all long gone and the building was heavily overgrown with ivy. The place for the sanctuary had a beautiful apse that was intact and provided a covering from sun and rain for the altar and organ that we had installed. I was also able to borrow four benches from a local church. With a thick covering of ivy on the walls inside and out, our little chapel was beautiful. In the evening those of us who had worked together to prepare our chapel met there and sang hymns and then prayed together before going back to our tents. From this point on, the chapel became a centre for quiet reflection and prayer by individuals and groups, and at their request I commenced a weekly service of Holy Communion on Wednesday mornings. I also began a routine of going up to the chapel early each morning for quiet reflection and prayer.

The divisional chaplains were planning a School of Church Membership during the summer so I introduced discussions with the men, in groups of platoon size, on the theme of "God and the war and the challenge of church membership." Many showed immediate interest. I had a long talk with Corporal Thwaites of the regimental aid post and with Private Ferguson, who was interested in being confirmed in the Anglican Church.

That month I had the good fortune to be named, along with Lieutenant Foster of the Pioneer Platoon, to accompany a party of seventy men from HQ Company and battalion HQ on a tour of Pompeii and Naples. On Friday, June 16, we got up at 0400 hours and left after an early breakfast. At Pompeii we were taken on a tour of the excavations of the ancient city, a fascinating experience. The city's streets were as they had been in 79 AD, with stepping stones for pedestrians and murals adorning many of the walls. We visited the Forum, the oldest amphitheatre in the Roman world, in which crowds of more than twenty thousand spectators could watch the gladiatorial contests. Approximately the size of a football field, it was situated in the centre of the city, surrounded by public buildings, many of which have survived. We also toured Pompeii's most impressive public structure, the Basilica, which served as a courtroom, a market, and a banking and trade centre. We then visited the temple of Apollo.

To round off our tour, we had a group picture taken on the steps of the Forum, copies of which were distributed to members of the tour. Our Italian guide, who had done a fair job of showing us the ancient city, seized the opportunity, while he had us all seated comfortably, to make a special pitch for his wife and little *bambinos* at home, who needed more than his meagre salary would provide, so would we each give him an additional fifty lira as he passed his hat around? We had had a good tour and were glad to rest our feet before returning to the vehicles. I think he probably got what he asked for.

On our way into Naples we passed by Vesuvius, which was smoking heavily from an eruption that had occurred a few months earlier. In places molten lava continued to flow from its sides. In Naples we were on our own and free to do as we wished. Lieutenant Foster and I had our lunch at the British Officer's Club then I had my hair cut, my shoes shined, and my picture taken by a street photographer.

We were fortunate to obtain tickets to see Verdi's *Rigoletto* at Teatro di San Carlo, the world-famous opera house. The only seats available were in the Royal Box, so we sat on lovely plush cushions and had a direct view of the stage. Mussolini and King Victor Emmanuel had frequently occupied the chairs we sat on. We also stood at the balustrade of the balcony from which Mussolini had delivered some of his speeches to the crowds gathered below during his glory days. This was my first experience of Italian opera. The singers were clearly pouring all their pent-up feelings at the tragedy that had so recently befallen their country into music. It was an unforgettable moment for me, and I determined to see as much Italian opera as possible while in that land.

On Monday, June 19, I was back at camp, discharging my usual duties. In the morning I attended a conference of the divisional chaplains at which we carried forward extensive plans for a Church Membership School to be held up in the mountains by beautiful Lake Metese. Men from all units of the 1st Canadian Division were invited to come for a final session of instruction and preparation before becoming a communicant member of a Protestant denomination of their choice.

After lunch, I was surprised to learn that I had been named to conduct approximately fifty men from the West Novas on a day trip to Rome, leaving early that evening. We set out at 1800 hours for Valmontone, where we camped for the night, continued on early the following morning, and arrived at Rome by 0830 hours. There we were invited to attend a special Mass of Thanksgiving to celebrate the liberation of the city. As I was the only officer present, I linked up with the orderly room sergeant and the regimental quartermaster sergeant, both of whom had expressed a wish to attend the services, one a United Church man, the other a Presbyterian, and myself an Anglican. There being no transportation in the city, it was a long walk, and we arrived as the service was about to commence. The Basilica di San Giovanni in Laterano (Church of St. John Lateran) seemed to be packed to the doors, but the usher, an English colonel, who had had an audience with the pope on the previous day, said there were seats up front and marched the three of us there. The service was conducted by the senior Roman Catholic chaplains of the 8th Army, the Royal Air Force, and the 1st Canadian Corps. The address, delivered by Father Carpenter on the text "Thou art Peter," was a clear reaffirmation of the popes' descent from the great apostle.

Vatican City was opened specially for Allied troops, so we caught a ride and went over. St. Peter's was a masterpiece of beauty and magnificence. We had a guide who explained every part of the church and who took us to see its treasures. From there we were led outside and re-entered the Vatican on the right side to gain the audience chambers. I was whisked up to the front of the chapel with the other officers, where we had an audience with Pope Pius XII. Speaking in English, the pope commented upon the number of Englishmen who had given their lives for the true faith in generations gone by. He then gave us his blessing, and we were all invited to go up and meet him and receive a special blessing.

After the service we walked down toward the Colosseum, its great walls still standing after almost two thousand years. Much of its marble facing had been removed, as had its marble floor, but its great walls and breastworks of stone and brick remained, with some of the steps still intact.

I sat high up in the stadium overlooking the arena and reflected on ancient times. There, on that spot before me, was shed the blood of early Christian martyrs. Over to the side, in an underground cavern with great iron bars, were the cages where the lions were kept in hunger, awaiting their prey. These great, brute beasts were just satisfying the needs of their bodies, but to the crowds that watched, a vast multitude grown weary from excessive pleasures and feasting, these Christians were just a new form of sport to give fleeting satisfaction to their jaded appetites.

I thought of the martyrs and of what faith they had that enabled them to remain stoic in the face of such mockery and allow themselves to be made a sport for pagans. Their cause must have seemed hopeless, given that they were challenging the mighty power and glittering worldliness of a proud and haughty empire. Yet, there they stood, alone and yet not alone, and shed their blood for Christ, whose presence and love mattered more to them than all the agonies that they were to endure. Gladly they died, and by their deaths they lit the torch of faith and freedom in the hearts of men and women. Had they been unwilling to stand alone for Christ, think what humanity would have missed, for the whole course of history was altered by their devotion unto death for the Master who had died for them. It occurred to me that we were at another great turning point of civilization, and that there was a similar call for men and women willing to stand alone, to make Christ king in their hearts and homes and the centre of their daily life and work.

From the Colosseum I walked across to the Palatine Hill to see the ruins of the palace of Caesar Augustus, who reigned during the time when our Lord was born. We also saw the Forum, still very well preserved, where the great discussions took place. I was impressed with the beautiful marble carvings and the great arches and pillars, and, even more so, to realize that these ancient rooms had been heated with steam, as had the baths. It was a solemn reminder of how easily all the glory and the good of a truly great civilization may be swept away and lost by generations of neglect and indifference.

Our tour concluded, we made our way back to the rendezvous point, where our cooks had supper waiting. Then we boarded our trucks and set out for camp, bivouacking overnight and arriving just in time for lunch.

On Saturday, July 8, I arranged an interview with the CO to express my concern at the serious venereal disease record of the West Novas. I had raised this problem with Ronnie soon after he arrived at our rest area, and sought his agreement to my speaking to the men in each company on the whole question of sex, but he at that time did not grasp the significance of the situation. Now, however, with the regiment facing a major problem, he agreed that I could speak about it in Padre's Hours.

Early on Sunday, July 4, we moved to a new area to prepare for a two-day Infantry/Tank exercise, with the realization that our peaceful days of rest and reorganization were drawing to a close and we would soon again be thrown into the maelstrom. After lunch I held the first in a series of platoon-strength Padre's Hours with No. 9 Platoon of A Company. I spoke about the part that our sexuality plays in the formation of our personalities and social relationships. I told the men that sexuality was one of God's greatest gifts, enabling men and women to unite in the production of a new human being. I spoke of the psychological bond that is formed between two human beings engaged in sexual intercourse, of the enriching and strengthening effect on them of a commitment to one another in a lifetime companionship. I also stressed that if a man who is thus committed to a wife at home has sexual intercourse with another woman, the bond between himself and his wife is broken. He has distanced himself from her and she will sense this in his communications with her, even though she may have no immediate knowledge of what he is doing. Finally, I spoke on the Christian standard of morals and the men's challenge to self-control as a preparation to return to their wives and girlfriends with clean bodies and pure minds. They listened intently and I think my message struck home. In conclusion, I pointed out the cleansing power of Christ to make them decent again and start them off afresh. After the discussion, I swam with them in a river that ran close at hand.

In the evening I brought the organ into an open field and started playing the old familiar tunes. In no time a group of twenty or thirty men gathered and we sang hymns together for almost two hours. During a break to rest our voices, I spoke on "The faith of a Christian." We then sang some more and closed with prayers for absent friends, repeated the Lord's Prayer, and closed with that familiar evening prayer, "We will lay us down in peace and take our rest; for it is Thou, Lord, only that makest us to dwell in safety."

The following day tragedy struck one of our men in the peaceful Piedimonte d'Alife valley when Pte. Joseph Daniels drowned in the Volturno River while on a platoon exercise. We tried to locate the body but were unsuccessful. In the evening an officer from A Company invited me to bring the organ over to their lines for a song service. We set it up under a spreading tree, and more than half the company gathered around and sang their favourite songs and hymns. When it became dark, we stood in a circle and prayed for those we love and those who were absent, joined together in the Lord's Prayer, and closed with the evening prayer, "We will lay us down in peace and take our rest."

On Tuesday morning Private Daniels's body was retrieved from the river, and so on Wednesday I held a funeral service and buried him in the British Cemetery in Riardo.

During these weeks, many of the men had remarked in their personnel information cards that they would like to talk with the padre, and more were seeking interviews with me, so I spent Saturday morning chatting with many of them. That afternoon, after a number of interviews, I had

Chapter Five

an interesting chat with the new divisional educational officer, Sergeant Dempster, a schoolteacher from Brockville, Ontario, who informed me that my unit was more religiously inclined than any he had been in throughout the division. I'm sure he was correct. The evening was spent in preparation for the Sunday service. I got to bed at midnight. Eighteen-hour days were becoming normal for me as the only way I could cope with the demands on my time.

Four hundred men attended the Sunday service, and I was the organist. The organ had been damaged, but our Pioneer, Cpl. Gilbert Rafuse, repaired it. It was a great asset to the singing. I conducted interviews throughout the day, and in the evening I spoke in the little stone chapel on the meaning of membership in the Christian Church to men who wished to know more about the Church Membership School.

Later in the evening I had a long interview with a junior officer who declared that he was meeting with the CO to discuss his future in the army. He had joined the West Novas in January 1944, just one week before I was appointed their chaplain, and had served as a platoon commander ever since. Of the twenty-five infantry reinforcement officers who arrived at that time, he was the sole remaining lieutenant. The others had either been killed in action, wounded and sent out, or promoted. During that six-month period he had been engaged in all the battles in which the West Novas had been involved, including patrol activity along the Arielli front throughout the winter, the follow-through from the Gustav Line, the fight through the Hitler Line, and the Melfa River battles. He believed he had done his stint as a platoon commander, and if he was ever going to be promoted he thought it should come now, prior to further engagement with the enemy.

It was evident to him, he declared, that with the general optimism that the war would soon be over, there would be strong pressure brought to bear upon front-line commanding officers to accept captains from rear echelon who wanted to get battle experience before the war ended. Unless action was taken to forestall this pressure, men who had borne the heat and burden of battle for the past months would be passed over. He felt the CO should either promote him now or court-martial him for insubordination and presumably cashier him. I listened intently to his problem, and assured him that I was interested in his concern and would hold myself in readiness for further consultation with him or with the CO if he so wished.

On Wednesday evening the CO summoned me in to discuss the junior officer's rather unusual request that he be sent to a psychiatrist for examination. I had found the officer to be a practical realist in working with the men in his platoon and suggested to the CO that his request was reasonable. He had demonstrated leadership in the three separate actions in which

I had observed him as I moved about the regiment, and I felt that if he was ever going to be promoted it should be soon. Ronnie asked me to seek a further conversation with the officer and to advise him accordingly.

On Thursday, July 20, I set out at 0600 hours with seventy-five West Novas for the Church Membership School up in the mountains, just above beautiful Lake Metese. Hundreds of men attended the one-day school, organized by the Protestant chaplains of 1st Canadian Division. The plenary opening session was addressed by Lt. Col. J. Logan-Vencta, deputy assistant Protestant chaplain from Ottawa, following which the men went to areas designated for each of the denominations represented, for a series of discussions introduced and conducted by Unit Chaplains of their denominational choice. I had the privilege of introducing a discussion for Anglican candidates on "The Baptismal Covenant," emphasizing the personal nature and importance of the commitment into which they were entering. My task was to provide an overview of subjects to be dealt with during the day: the threefold blessing that Christians receive from God in becoming a member of Christ, a child of God, and an inheritor of the Kingdom of Heaven; and the corresponding threefold commitment Christians must make to resist all forms of evil, to believe in God, and to strive to respond to God's call upon our time and energy day by day.

It was a beautiful day for our outdoor school and the discussions and programs went as planned. A grand total of 606 men prepared themselves to become active members of the Church of Christ in various denominations while serving in the army in the midst of the chaos of war. Thirty-five of those entering the Anglican Church of Canada were baptized in preparation for their confirmation. The Baptists were led by their chaplain down to the waters of Lake Metese to be baptized by immersion. Maj. J. I. McKinney, Senior Chaplain, 1st Canadian Division, addressed the concluding plenary session on church unity, comparing the various denominations to the different regiments in the same army. We arrived back at camp by 2000 hours.

On Sunday we drove up to Rome to be on hand for the confirmation on Monday. Having the morning free, I joined Major Durnford and Captain Daniels for a tour of the old city, including a visit to the prison in which St. Paul is said to have spent most of his time while in Rome, and where he wrote several of his letters while he was awaiting execution. We then went to the Pantheon, a beautiful round building built by Agrippa in 27 BC as a memorial to all the gods, and one of the finest specimens of classical Roman architecture. From there we went to the Catacombs of St. Calixtus, great underground dwellings where the early Christians buried their dead and lived in hiding during times of persecution. This was a memorable experience, to walk along the corridors and read the inscriptions on the walls, some of which dated back to very early Christian times. We made a brief visit to the Roman Forum and to the Forum of Augustus, and then visited the cemetery where the English poet John Keats lies buried.

In the afternoon we gathered at All Saints Anglican Church in Rome for the confirmation service conducted by the Bishop of Lichfield, England, who confirmed 250 candidates. All had been prepared at the school and a few, including four West Novas, had also been privately prepared by their chaplains. Immediately following the confirmation, the bishop held a service of Holy Communion for the men, their first, before they had to return to their regiments.

The regiment was on the alert for a move when we arrived back at camp, but I arranged a meeting with the newly confirmed men on the evening of Wednesday, July 26, in the chapel, where I spoke to them on the service of Holy Communion.

I reminded the confirmands that a sacrament is an outward and visible sign of an inward and spiritual grace, and in Holy Communion the outward and visible signs are the bread and wine over which are repeated the words of our Lord at his last meal with his disciples. In receiving the spiritual grace of Communion our lives are renewed. Receiving into ourselves the living presence of Christ refreshes us for the spiritual warfare in which we are engaged. Christ accompanies us as we undertake the varied and difficult tasks that are laid upon us in the ordeal of war, and which we would continue until we defeated the enemy.

The men knew by this time that our halcyon days were over and that in a couple of days we would have to leave behind our beautiful and peaceful ivy-covered chapel in the Piedimonte d'Alife valley and move north to re-engage the enemy. They felt prepared for whatever lay before them.

CHAPTER SIX

Preparing for the Attack

July–August 1944

Piedimonte d'Alife / Assisi / Modino / Jesi / Foglia River

On Saturday, July 29, we broke camp and set out again. The day before our departure, knowing we would be on the move, I had spent an hour and a half in meditation in the little chapel, before removing the pews and returning all our borrowed equipment to the priest in town—to his great surprise, for he had not expected to see it again.

We headed north, through Rome and out on the Via Flaminia, our first destination being Castelina where we spent several days. While there the commanding officer addressed each company on the role the regiment was to play in the forthcoming battles to break the Gothic Line, a series of strongly built defensive positions running roughly from Pesaro on the east coast of Italy, through Florence, to the west coast in the vicinity of Pisa.

Following the Allied breakthrough at the Liri Valley and the retreat north of Rome, the German forces, under the leadership of Field Marshal Kesselring, had conducted a series of delaying actions to provide time for the military engineers of the Todt Organization to complete the construction of these defensive positions. He was pursued by the American 5th Army, under Gen. Mark Clark, on the left, and the British 8th Army, commanded by Lt. Gen. Sir Oliver Leese, on the right. By early August the German forces had retreated to the outer defences of the Gothic Line, and it was General Alexander's plan to feint in front of Florence to confirm the enemy in their thinking that the attack would come in that area. To this end we broke camp on Monday, August 7, and moved by transport to the high ground overlooking Florence, where we remained for forty-eight hours. We had an excellent view of the city directly across the river from our camp, but I saw little of it for I suffered an attack of dysentery that kept me on my back most of the time we were there.

Chapter Six

On Wednesday, August 9, the regiment moved by transport to a staging area near Siena, and on the following day to Perugia, where we spent approximately ten days. My driver, Dennis, arrived with my truck, and I had the luxury of a bed to sleep in and an office where I could work. To my great surprise I was at this time assigned a second batman, who would be free to accompany me when we went into action. He was Private Johnson from D Company, who had been discovered to be only seventeen years of age. Application had been made to have him struck off strength, a process that might take a few weeks, so during the wait he was to serve as my assistant.

A further surprise was an offer to spend two days at Assisi. I set out in my truck early on the morning of Tuesday, August 15, with my driver and batman and rations for the day. We first visited the Basilica di Santa Maria degli Angeli (St. Mary of the Angels), a large church that encloses a tiny chapel, known as the Porziuncula, which is said to have been rebuilt by St. Francis, and to be where he died. A monk guided us around St. Mary's and also interpreted the many paintings on the walls. Here I met a Lieutenant Doran of No. 17 Special Employment Company and learned from him that Jim Claxton, whom I had met while at No. 4 Base, was near at hand. I had lunch with Jim at No. 17 and we spent the afternoon together.

We visited many places in the city associated with St. Francis and his movement, including the Church of St. Clare and the Convent of St. Damian, which became the early headquarters of the Franciscan movement and also home of the Order of Poor Clares. At the Church of St. Francis we were guided by an Irish monk, Father Gaff, and we spent the balance of the afternoon touring the huge edifice and its galleries, the walls of which are covered with murals by Giotto and other famous painters. We remained for vespers and, it being the Feast of the Assumption, found ourselves attending Mass in the central church, a rare occurrence. I was deeply impressed with the peaceful, devotional atmosphere pervading the place.

Afterwards we had supper, prepared by our two young cooks, on the lawn beside the truck. As we sat down to eat, two Sisters who had attended the service passed by on their way to the convent and inquired if we would like a bottle of wine, so we ended up dining in style. After dinner we went to No. 17 Special Employment Company, where we had been invited to spend the night. I had a good discussion that evening with two officers on the significance of Christianity and the Church today. One of them confessed that he had not been able to speak the name of Christ blasphemously since being in action, for he had felt the presence of God with him there.

On Wednesday we were off again to Assisi. We took a scenic route into the city, did some shopping, and picked up a guide to show us around the

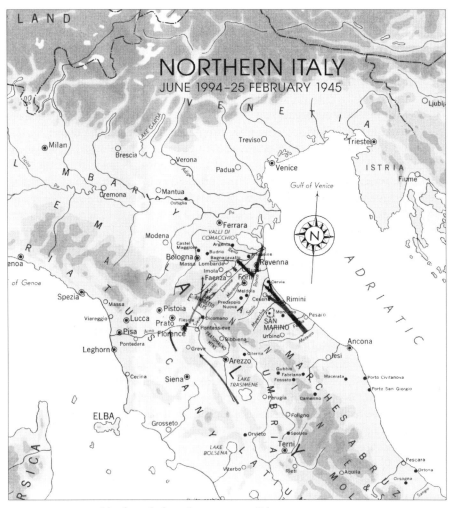

Northern Italy, 10 June 1944 – 25 February 1945

Rocca, a medieval castle that overlooks the Umbrian plains below. Here the guide showed us the passageways and observation posts the Germans had built during their occupation of Assisi.

After some more sightseeing we returned to No. 17 for lunch and a swim. We returned to camp by 1600 hours for supper and the weekly discussion group. Our attention was given to the passage in the Gospel of Matthew where Jesus challenges his disciples to believe that God really cares for each and every one of them, to place their faith in God. The chapter concludes: "Do not be anxious about tomorrow; tomorrow will look

CHAPTER SIX

after itself. Each day has troubles enough of its own" (Matthew 6:34). This final verse elicited lively discussion as the men knew that each day brought them that much nearer to the ordeal of battle and its consequences. What a contrast between the peace and quiet of the churches associated with the little saint of Assisi and the chaos into which these men were moving in the line of duty!

I spent Thursday catching up with work, and on Friday the CO held an orders group, following which we prepared to move. My truck went back to B Echelon and all badges and markings on personnel and vehicles were removed. Before my truck departed I distributed to the men of the four rifle companies packages of cigarettes from friends at home that I had been storing up for just this purpose. At 1745 hours on Saturday, August 19, we set out by transport and moved over the mountains to Jesi, near the Adriatic coast. Here the CO briefed the regiment on the forthcoming offensive and the men got ready for battle.

During the following week of preparations, I took every opportunity to meet with the men of the rifle companies and take their minds off the grim business ahead by discussing their plans for rehabilitation after the war. On Thursday, August 24, I rose early and went into a cornfield, where I spent an hour and a half alone in prayer for the regiment, the CO, the officers, the men, and for myself, that I might be ready for whatever part I should be called upon to play. In conversations with Ronnie and with Brigadier Bernatchez I had agreed that the normal place for the chaplain during action was at the regimental aid post, to meet and speak with the wounded as they came through. I recognized that in the battle at the Hitler Line, and others before it, I had responded to urgent calls for assistance and had become very involved in bringing out the wounded, with the result that I had had some very close calls. Both the CO and the brigadier pointed out to me that there was only one chaplain in the regiment and each in turn urged me to remain at the regimental aid post during future action. Taking these conversations very much to heart, I prayed constantly for guidance in knowing where my real responsibilities lay. My concern was for the welfare of the men, whether in or out of battle, and it was not always easy to see where I should be or what I should do in particular situations as they arose.

Early that evening the regiment set out by a long, hard march along a goat path to a staging area near Modino, led by Maj. Bill Thexton, the officer commanding A Company. I set out on the march with D Company and gradually worked my way up to the front of the column, visiting with the men as I went. It turned out to be a seventeen-mile march, a little longer than expected. We arrived at 0345 hours. I had a sponge bath and got to bed at 0400 hours. I slept until 0700 hours on Friday, August 25, and awoke refreshed. That evening the CO held an orders group and briefed us on the forthcoming battle. First and 2nd Brigades were to cross the Metauro River at midnight and engage the enemy with 3rd Brigade in reserve.

On Saturday, August 26, the regiment set out at 0930 hours on route march to a new area. We learned that the attack had gone well, that the enemy had offered little resistance and were pulling back. At that time awards to the regiment for its action in the Hitler Line battles were announced. The CO and three platoon sergeants received decorations and were congratulated by Brigadier Bernatchez. As Major Thexton, in his account of this, remarked, "it was rather a Spartan sprinkling of awards considering the West Novas were the first Unit to break through the Hitler Line." That night I got to bed early, but could not sleep because of indigestion! Was this the effect of our guns firing directly behind us every half hour or so? I finally slept until 0700 hours, and then spent some time reading the latest information from Ottawa on rehabilitation preparations. At 1800 hours we were on the march again to a destination seven miles north, an assembly area where the German army had been just a few days before. We prepared for imminent action.

I spent all of Monday, August 28, conducting Communion services for small groups of men throughout the camping area. Several of these were held in vineyards whose vines were heavy with ripe grapes, and the men knelt on the bare ground to receive the wafer of bread and sip of wine that was a pledge to each of the living of the Presence of One who would be with them throughout their ordeal. It must be remembered that none of these men wanted war. They longed for peace, but had been caught up by the ordeal of the ages, and could not hope for peace until they had finished the job in which they were immersed. That night I slept on my camp cot beside an Italian barn, as I had done the night before, awaiting the call forward, which could come at any moment.

On Tuesday, August 29, the rifle company commanders, Maj. Alan Nicholson, Maj. Bill Thexton, Capt. Harvey Jones, and Capt. Stanley Smith, went forward at short notice to make a reconnaissance of the area held by the 48th Highlanders of 1st Brigade. They commanded the heights above the Foglia River valley, on the far side of which the enemy forces occupied strongpoints in the main Gothic Line defences. Here the company commanders were briefed by the CO, after which they left for a reconnaissance of the areas they were to take over from the 48th Highlanders. Meanwhile, the rifle companies had left by route march for the forward area, and by midnight the relief of the 48th Highlanders was complete.

During the night of August 29–30, patrols from C and D Companies made a reconnaissance of the river line approaches and crossings, and the nearest mines were found to be approximately three hundred yards north of the river. They also reported that the river was fordable throughout our area. Further reconnaissance, however, disclosed that the area was not suitable to move into during daylight, as it was under enemy observation. At 1330 hours, Wednesday, August 30, two Italian civilians were interrogated by the Intelligence officer. They stated that the enemy had retired across the river two days previously, and that the area across the river was heavily mined. An ominous silence fell over the area for the rest of the day, with no shelling or mortaring and no evident movement of enemy troops. What did this mean? Was the enemy preparing for a counterattack, or were they, as reported by some informants, pulling back from these prepared positions?

At 1400 hours an orders group was held at battalion headquarters, which was situated in a small stone barn overlooking the river valley. Bill Thexton, the officer commanding A Company, states in his account that when the company commanders arrived the CO, Lieutenant Colonel Waterman, was speaking to the brigade commander, Bernatchez, on the field telephone and that, after listening for a rather long time, "we heard him say, 'But, Sir, my regiment will be massacred, at least give me some tanks.' After further listening to the brigade commander, the Colonel replied, 'Very good, Sir' and hung up." In the Brigade War Diary it refers to this conversation and states that Lieutenant Colonel Waterman had asked for a squadron of tanks and requested that he might send two companies forward instead of one in the initial advance. There is no mention of the minefields. His request was refused.

Without referring to this conversation, the CO gave his orders for an immediate attack on the Gothic Line. B Company, commanded by Capt. Harvey Jones, was to attack and secure point 133, square 0277, after which the remaining rifle companies would move forward on the CO's orders and secure a bridgehead across the Foglia River. There would be no supporting fire and the attack would take place in daylight.

To continue the account by Thexton:

> At 1600 hours, B Company crossed the start line, A, C, and D Companies formed up on the top of the hill ready to follow them. It was a fascinating and awesome sight to see this small group of men moving in extended order down the steep hill to the valley below in full view of the enemy. They looked like ants as they crossed the Foglia River and disappeared into the underbrush on the far side. At 1640 hours, B Company ran into the minefield and, unable to find a route through or around it, continued a cautious advance. At 1717 hours, B Company came under enemy small arms fire and suffered several casualties from Schu mines. Having reached the lateral road, they came under heavy

small arms and mortar fire and, despite numerous efforts to push forward, they were forced to consolidate their position in the anti-tank ditch several hundred yards south of the lateral road.

According to my records for that day, while the rifle companies had been moved forward on the evening of August 29, there were elements of other companies engaged in the route march throughout the next morning. I distinctly remember watching a young man sketch a town on a hill off to our right as he ate his lunch that morning. Several weeks later, when I was visiting the wounded in hospital, I came across him busily painting a picture of the town from his pencil sketch of that morning. According to my recollections, recorded shortly afterwards, I continued marching with the troops on August 30 and arrived at the West Novas' position along the high hills overlooking the Foglia River valley around 1600 hours. After locating the regimental aid post and depositing my pack and kit, I went on to locate tactical HQ and fill myself in on the situation.

Chapter Seven

Tragedy at Foglia River

August 30–31, 1944

Foglia River / Gothic Line

Another battle was in the offing when I arrived at battalion HQ late in the afternoon of Wednesday, August 30. I located the regimental aid post, deposited my pack and kit, and made my way over to the tiny stone barn that was serving as tactical HQ to learn what our next move might be. Capt. Harvey Jones, the officer commanding B Company, was reporting over the field radio the results of his company's reconnaissance across the Foglia River. He and his men had crossed the river without incident and made their way up to an anti-tank ditch without encountering enemy action. As they approached the lateral road several hundred yards in front of the ditch, they came under heavy fire, which disclosed enemy forces in depth with strong firepower from machine guns located on the flanking hills, backed up by artillery and mortar fire. The enemy had demolished the little village and had constructed strongpoints across the front. They suffered a number of casualties, including one officer killed, and withdrew to the anti-tank ditch.

On hearing the report, all present, except apparently the CO, considered the situation called for support from artillery, tanks, and supporting infantry. The artillery forward observation officer indicated that his men could blast the strongpoints ahead of the advancing infantry. The tank liaison officer pointed out on the map the excellent opportunity for tank support up the road that led directly from the river to the battalion objective. Since the attack was not going in until first light there would be ample time for the engineers to clear the anti-tank mines from the road, and as Captain Jones had secured the bridge over the anti-tank ditch, there would be nothing to prevent them from accompanying the infantry as they went in.

The CO, however, rejected all offers of assistance, declaring that the infantry did not need them. "This is the infantry's day," he blustered. "We will show you how wars should be fought and won. We don't need the artillery and we don't need the tanks. This is our day!" To this day I have difficulty interpreting these words. Was Ronnie being facetious, putting on an act? Was he maintaining a bold front in the face of an impossible assignment? He was a born actor and was quite capable of doing so. And I had not been present earlier in the afternoon to hear him expostulating on the telephone. But, surely this was a new situation that called for a reconsideration of whatever orders had been given previously. We will never know why he did not make a new decision in light of the report.

In any event, I was shocked, and I could not believe what my ears were hearing. I wondered where the brigadier was, and why someone else did not contravene this decision. On other such occasions, during the approach to the Hitler Line and throughout that battle, Brigadier Bernatchez had always been present when crucial decisions had to be made. But he was nowhere to be seen, and there did not appear to be anyone else present with the authority to question the CO's decision. I had difficulty believing that Ronnie meant what he said. But I knew him well enough to be aware that once he had committed himself to a plan of action he would not alter it unless ordered to do so. That he was in earnest became clear without delay, for he immediately gave orders for the rifle companies to prepare to descend the valley, cross the river, and dig in. D and C Companies were to attack at first light under Maj. Alan Nicholson and Capt. Stanley Smith.

After all the infantry/tank exercises of the past summer, it seemed, absurdly, that the men were to be sent in to break into the main Gothic Line defences without any artillery preparation or supporting armour. I feared disaster and felt helpless to do anything to prevent it. As a chaplain I could not attempt in any way to interfere with the conduct of a battle. So what could I do? I pondered the situation as I made my way back to the regimental aid post. By the time I arrived, it was clear what I must do. I informed Corporal Thwaites at the regimental aid post that I was going along with the two companies and asked him to prepare a small pack with shell dressings and all necessary first-aid equipment. He filled my canteen with fresh water and I set out to join C and D Companies in descending the Foglia valley.

If anyone had asked me why I was going, or what I thought I could do, I could not have given an answer. I had no idea what I might be able to accomplish by going, except to be with the men. I went because I could do nothing else. My resolution to remain at the regimental aid post dissolved in the face of what I felt was going to be a disaster. I went because the presence of him who had called me into the ministry in 1925, and had urged me to offer my services as a chaplain in 1940, was directing me to this route. Like Abraham of old, I went out not knowing whither I was going or what I

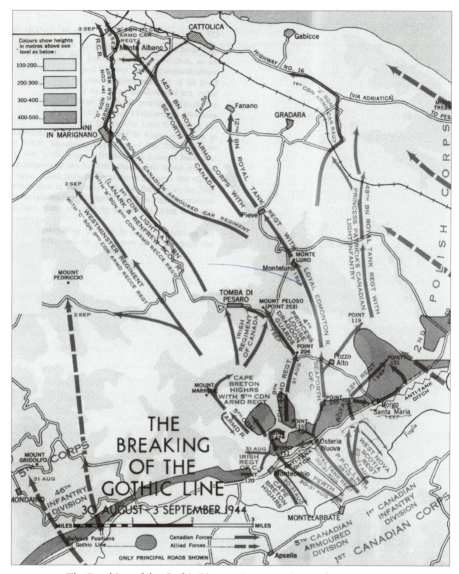

The Breaking of the Gothic Line, 30 August–3 September 1944

could do in the situation, but convinced that the presence of Christ was with me.

I arrived at the brow of the hill just as C and D Companies started down the face of the cliff to descend into the valley. We made our way down a winding path and crossed the river without incident. The river was a mere trickle. I did not even get my feet wet, crossing on rocks in the riverbed. We moved forward to the left to an opening in a stand of trees, where we dug in for the night. There was sporadic shelling, but no one was injured. It was a sleepless night. I remember enjoying the tot of rum that each of us received to keep us warm in our slit trenches. I wrapped myself in my gas cape and pondered the situation, praying that I might be up to the challenge of whatever lay before me. Although I could not envisage the ordeal ahead, I was sure this was where I was intended to be.

At approximately 0200 hours on Thursday, August 31, Maj. Alan Nicholson called an orders group at which he informed us that he and Capt. Stan Smith had just returned from an orders group of the company commanders with the CO, held at tactical HQ, at which they had received the battle plan. It was a grim picture. The attack was to go in at first light from the anti-tank ditch occupied by B Company, without any prior artillery preparation and without supporting armour. D Company was to lead off, followed by C Company two minutes later, in an attempt to dislodge the enemy from their defensive positions. Major Nicholson stated that he personally disagreed with the manner in which the attack was laid on. To make matters worse, Capt. Harvey Jones reported at the orders group that the enemy had been out all evening laying mines across the forward area. The CO did not appear to listen to what Jones said, gave no indication that he even heard him, and took no steps to cope with this new aspect of the situation. Major Nicholson feared the attack would be a disaster and personally did not wish to undertake it as presently planned. But, if he were to refuse, it would mean that some other officer, without the benefit of such information as he had, would be required to lead the men. Under the circumstances, he felt he must accept the responsibility of command, and asked all present for their support.

I went back to my slit trench and spent the remaining hours of the darkness pondering the immediate future and trying to think how I might be of some assistance. My worst fears had now been confirmed. The attack was to go ahead as announced, in broad daylight, without any supporting fire, and with the added hazard of a minefield. Awakened before daylight and ready to move off at 0530 hours, I marched in with Major Nicholson. As we approached the anti-tank ditch, he suggested that the stretcher-bearers and myself remain in the ditch with B Company, and be ready to come forward when called.

Before the attack, the two companies lined up along the lip of the ditch, C Company behind D Company, and each man fired a clip of ammunition in the direction of the enemy strongpoints, thereby destroying any element of surprise that might have been possible. The men reloaded, and D Company went over the top of the ditch and moved forward towards their objective, which was point 133 on the Gothic Line. They were followed one minute later by C Company. There was no reaction from the enemy until the advancing troops reached the minefield. As soon as the mines started going off, the enemy opened up with machine-gun fire from the adjoining hills on both flanks, accompanied by a barrage of shells and mortars. Immediately there were urgent cries for help, for stretcher-bearers, and the padre, from every section of the front.

It was agonizing to hear the cries of the wounded. Some of them had lost their feet from Schu mines, others had been wounded by machine-gun fire, or by the shells and mortars that were coming thick and fast. I have never felt so helpless in all my life as on that occasion, and I wondered what I could possibly do to help in the face of such a tragedy. Suddenly three young men approached me, stretcher-bearers for C and D Companies, with Alvin Hastings, stretcher-bearer for B Company, as their spokesman. Hastings asked me to come and speak with his company commander, Capt. Harvey Jones, and try to persuade him to let them to go out with stretchers to attend to the wounded men and bring them in. Captain Jones had already refused their request, saying it would be suicidal to go out. I voiced some concern, but Hastings assured me that he had carrying parties ready to go, so I agreed to see what I could do, relieved at the possibility of finding a way to respond to the cries for help.

Captain Jones was an officer with extensive experience in battle, and he was adamant in his conviction that it would be suicidal to go out. He further protested that he would have to send an officer with the stretcher-bearers, and he was not prepared to do that. I said that, as an officer, I was prepared to lead the carrying parties. He replied that he would not take the responsibility of allowing the men to go out into that kind of flak. He simply could not permit them to go. I suggested that the decision needn't be his, and said, "You have a telephone, phone the CO and let him decide. It was he who sent the men into the hell they are in; perhaps he will now accept responsibility for allowing the stretcher-bearers to go out to help the wounded and bring them back." Jones called the CO, who said he thought the padre was a fool to even consider such a rash act, but had no control over him. He would permit anyone who wished to accompany me to do so, but the decision was up to each man. No one was being ordered into that situation.

Each stretcher-bearer had his carrying party present, so I turned and asked them, "Are we all here?" They responded as with one voice, "We're all here, ready to go." "All right," I said, "follow me. We will go in single file to make a smaller target." I climbed over the lip of the ditch, followed by the carrying parties, and set out for the forward area. As soon as we got out of

Chapter Seven

the ditch we were mortared heavily, and the men in the forward area shouted at us to get down, as we were drawing fire. We were already down and waited while the mortars exploded harmlessly all around us.

While the mortars were whining their way in our direction, I had looked around and found a small willow switch, which I cut off with my army knife and trimmed to a good length. When the shelling was over, I pulled the red-cross flag from my thigh pocket, pinned it to the willow stick, raised it high, then stood up, and waved to the men to follow. The stretcher-bearers, each of whom had a similar flag in his pocket, followed suit, and we moved forward with no direct fire from the enemy. Our flags had been recognized and the enemy observed the rules of the Geneva Convention. We soon arrived at the minefield. I had no difficulty detecting where the mines were. I stopped at the first one and showed the men how to recognize them by the disturbance of the grass and dust on the leaves. I urged each man to forget the enemy and keep his eyes fixed on the ground while crossing the field to avoid becoming a casualty himself.

We soon reached the area of desolation. It was a strip plotted out by the enemy as a prepared killing ground across the line of attack. Our men were lying in every direction on the ground, some dead, others in agony and calling for help. All the officers in both companies had been either killed or wounded, including the two company commanders, each of whom had lost a leg in the minefield. The three stretcher-bearers went to work on the most serious cases. We began the arduous task of carrying the wounded out of the minefield, at first using our route into the area, but later we decided to move forward a few yards to the lateral road, proceed to the crossroads, and turn south down the paved road leading to battalion HQ. The usual carrying party consisted of four persons, the stretcher-bearer and three carriers. But here, with a long distance to cover and so many wounded needing immediate attention, it was imperative that the stretcher-bearers continue working with the wounded.

I became the fourth person on one stretcher. We recruited two others from those who had not been wounded and started the long haul, a kilometre or more, under the intense heat of an Italian August sun, back to a clump of willows north of the river, where the regimental aid post jeep ambulance met us. As soon as I could be relieved from carrying for a spell, I walked about, seeking to bring as much comfort as possible to the wounded, assisting in dressing and binding up wounds. Those who had lost a lot of blood urgently needed water to wet their parched lips and relieve their terrible thirst. I had to insist upon only a sip of water for each, but, despite rationing, my bottle was soon empty.

Some forty men had lost feet from Schu mines, while others had received wounds from machine-gun, shell, or mortar fire, or by shrapnel

from S mines. Some were entangled in barbed wire and surrounded by mines. One young man, whom I shall never forget, lay tangled in wire and wounded by both mines and shrapnel. He called out to me as I approached, "Padre, for God's sake, don't come near me, the place is loaded with mines. Someone has to stay alive to return and tell the people at home what hell they sent us into." I replied that I hoped, by God's grace, to live through this, but that now we needed to get him out of there and carry him back to safety. It was a sticky situation, to cut the wire and bind up his wounds, all the while stepping around Schu mines. We did manage to get him out and carry him back, but I doubt that he survived.

It was a painfully slow process, with only three stretchers and a long, hot carry, to bring out between sixty and seventy badly wounded men to where the carrier ambulance could pick them up and bring them back to the regimental aid post. Throughout the morning we were the only people allowed to move about with relative freedom. Anyone else, including an officer who came up to investigate the situation, had to crawl on his stomach under cover of the low shrubs. Around mid-morning those remaining from the decimated companies were withdrawn under cover of smoke, and the Royal 22nd Regiment was moved up to within five hundred yards behind the anti-tank ditch to safeguard against the possibility of a surprise counter-attack.

There was sporadic enemy shelling throughout this manoeuvre, and as the withdrawing troops reached a crossroads by the river used as a staging area for the vehicles evacuating the wounded, the enemy laid on a deadly barrage of artillery fire. It was designed to catch the troops as they moved through a cutting in the bank, and it was timed exactly. By good luck the regimental aid post ambulance had just left with its load of wounded, and fortunately for all of us, the barrage fell about twenty feet short. As we lay in the shallow ditches on either side of the road shrapnel sliced across to the south bank a few inches above us. It then lifted and came down again about twenty feet beyond the cutting. The young bamboo forest was completely shredded, but there were no casualties.

I returned again to the forward area and became frightfully concerned at the slow pace of the evacuation. As I passed through the lines of the Royal 22nd Regiment I noticed a soldier with a large red cross painted on his steel helmet. Walking over to within hailing distance, I asked him if he could bring a stretcher and carrying party and assist us. He shrugged his shoulders and waved his hands in a gesture that suggested he did not understand. I repeated my request and noticed this time that two other young men with him were interpreting my message. To my great relief, he responded, "Ouai, the Padre of the West Novas! Ouai." In no time he and his two companions were following us up to the minefield, and they continued carrying out the wounded until the job was completed. He was a young French Canadian who was afterwards awarded the Military Medal for his actions on behalf of his fellow Canadians of a sister regiment.

I couldn't help but reflect that had the CO accepted the offer of the tank liaison officer, the road would have been cleared of anti-tank mines, allowing the regimental aid post ambulance jeep to come within a few yards of where the majority of the casualties lay, and reducing by at least two-thirds the time required to get the wounded out.

Finally, after what seemed an endless effort, all the wounded we had located were evacuated, except one young man who had been shot through the sternum. He was determined to walk out, but I persuaded him, with great difficulty, against doing so, lest he cause himself more damage. I waited with him in the forward area until a stretcher could be brought back. During the wait, I walked about and obtained the names of eleven or twelve of the dead. Some had in their wallets the pink card they received in July for attendance at the Church Membership School, indicating they had become communicant members of a denomination.

During this lull in activity, while I awaited the stretcher and carrying party, I took some time out for my daily reading of a chapter from the New Testament. My reading on that day was chapter 6 of the Book of Revelation, which tells of the Seer's vision of the Four Horsemen of the Apocalypse, and the death and destruction that resulted from their release on the earth. The account seemed such an apt description of what we were experiencing that I read it aloud to the wounded man, and we briefly discussed the theme and its application to a world then at war.

Finally the stretcher party arrived. It had been intercepted by a German scouting party on its way in, but on seeing that they were going in for a casualty, the Germans allowed them to proceed. We walked directly past the spot on our way back, but met no interference. Some hundred yards before we reached the anti-tank ditch, a couple of men from B Company, seeing us walking down the road unmolested by enemy fire, climbed onto the bridge to look around. They were immediately shelled and one was slightly wounded before he could scurry into the ditch. The enemy was holding their fire while we evacuated our wounded, but they were alert.

At the river, we were picked up by the jeep ambulance and transported to the regimental aid post. So ended the most remarkable day of my life! I had difficulty believing that I was actually alive at the end of it. It had been too much to hope that our carrying parties could come through the kind of flak they encountered from 0600 hours until mid-morning, when the remaining troops were withdrawn. Afterwards an eerie silence fell over the area as I walked about, always with my flag flying, caring for the wounded and examining the dead to make sure there was no life remaining in them.

We left the dead to be brought out on the following day when the enemy had withdrawn. At least they were suffering no pain.

I was exhausted when I arrived at the regimental aid post and the doctor gave me a pill to enable me to get some sleep. I lay down and reflected upon the events of the past twenty-four hours. I thanked God for helping us to get the wounded out without becoming casualties ourselves. I finally slept and awoke refreshed quite early on the following morning, Friday, September 1. The CO requested an interview so I went over to tactical HQ. Ronnie was very subdued, as well he should have been after such a debacle, especially as the authorities had laid the responsibility squarely upon his shoulders. He told me there were two men missing, and he wondered if perhaps we had missed them in our search of the battlefield. Would I mind going out into the forward area, accompanied by a stretcher-bearer, and search to see if someone had been overlooked? I said I did not wish to go into the minefield, let alone take someone else with me, until the whole area had been swept for mines. After all the disturbance and milling about the day before it would be difficult to detect the mines by sight. He promised to have the whole area swept that morning. I agreed to go out at noon with some Pioneers who were going out to pick up weapons and equipment from the battlefield. The rest of the morning I spent plotting out a cemetery for men killed in the battle. Their bodies were brought out during the morning and early afternoon and we prepared them for burial.

I set out at noon with Victor Newell, a stretcher-bearer who had done a magnificent job the day before, and together we thoroughly searched the area, but to no avail. As we were about to return to the regimental aid post, Newell noticed a rifle up-ended in the midst of some shrubs, an area that had not been searched, and suggested we examine the spot. I agreed, but insisted he walk in my steps to make doubly sure of not stepping on a mine. As we moved towards the spot, Newell noticed a Tommy gun lying to our left. He asked if it would be all right for him to take just one step aside to retrieve it. Before I could reply there was an explosion that knocked me head over heels, covering the back of my head and neck with dirt. Newell had stepped on a Schu mine. His foot was blown off at the ankle.

The blast of these mines is such a shock to the system that there is little or no immediate bleeding. I had no difficulty in binding up the stump of his leg. With the help of the Pioneers, we laid him on a stretcher, loaded him onto the jeep ambulance, and sent him back, while I completed the search. I found no one. Newell was taken immediately to the field hospital, where the doctors operated on his leg for what seemed to be a straightforward wound. However, shortly after being wheeled back to his ward Newell died. An autopsy revealed that a small piece of metal from the toe of his army boot had entered his chest under the rib cage and penetrated his heart. Learning of this tragedy was a tremendous blow to me. Newell had been one of the heroes of the evacuation of the day before and had come through the whole ordeal unscathed. Now he was dead from a Schu mine in the very area where one day earlier he had walked about freely attending to the wounded.

As for the two missing men, a few days later I remembered my encounter with the young French-Canadian stretcher-bearer. It turned out that his two interpreters were West Novas who apparently found the flak too much and accepted their friend's invitation to share his dugout as the remnants of the two companies were being withdrawn. I have always hoped that the two West Novas returned to their own lines, but reflecting on this experience then and through the years since, I wondered if they were the two who were missing that morning.

After more than fifty years I still find myself asking how this disaster at the Foglia River crossing could have occurred. This was a major tragedy, with all the officers and senior NCOs and 50 percent of the men of two companies either killed or wounded. It also signalled the end of the career of a soldier who, as commanding officer of the West Nova Scotia Regiment, had given outstanding leadership throughout the spring offensive. The West Novas had distinguished themselves by being the first regiment to break through the Hitler Line. For his outstanding leadership in that action, the CO, Lt. Col. R.S.E. Waterman, had been awarded the Distinguished Service Order. What went wrong on August 30–31, 1944? It is evident that the CO had received orders to try to break through the main Gothic Line defences without any preparatory artillery fire or supporting armour. But that order had been given in the absence of information about the enemy forces and, to test the wisdom of that plan, he had been requested to carry out a reconnaissance in depth to determine the strength and disposition of the enemy. The whole picture was completely changed by the report of Capt. Harvey Jones.

Captain Jones's report showed the enemy to be present in strength, and in strongly fortified positions, with plenty of firepower from machine guns, mortars, and artillery. The CO received this report, so why did he not telephone Brigade or Division or whoever had laid on the attack and ask for supporting firepower? Indeed, was it even necessary for him to seek the permission of his superiors? Apparently there is a notation in the brigade diary for that day indicating that the CO had discretionary powers to utilize such supporting firepower as he deemed necessary to the success of the attack. Why, then, didn't the CO accept the offers of both the artillery forward observation officer and the tank liaison officer? And why did he not heed Jones's warning at the orders group early in the morning of August 31 that the enemy had mined the area where the men would make their attack?

At that hour there was still ample time for the Pioneers or the Engineers to clear paths through the minefield. We will never know the answers to these questions.

Another question looms large: why was Brigadier Bernatchez not present at that fateful moment of decision on the afternoon of August 30, 1944? The brigade diary indicates that he was on duty at that time, although one would have expected him to be in contact with his CO in order to receive the report of the reconnaissance in depth that he had personally ordered. Brigadier Bernatchez made a point of speaking to me a few days after this disaster. He explained that, in an effort to investigate the eerie silence hanging over the Foglia valley on August 30, he had flown over the area in a small reconnaissance plane, which ran into trouble and was forced to make a crash landing. The pilot was successful in gliding back into friendly territory, but in the crash Bernatchez suffered a broken jaw, and at the time the decisions were being made at the West Novas' tactical HQ that afternoon, he was in a field hospital having his jaw wired together. According to the brigade diary, the plane crash took place one week after the Foglia River crossing, but it is evident that this notation is wrongly placed; the date given is probably that on which the brigadier's wires and stitches were removed. I distinctly recall the difficulty with which he spoke, the movement of his jaw being severely restricted by wires. He apologized for his absence on that occasion, assuring me that had he been present things would have been ordered differently.

General Allard, who was then the CO of the Royal 22nd Regiment, states in his memoirs that Bernatchez asked him to go over and investigate the situation immediately after the tragedy. On arrival at Waterman's command post, he found that the CO was "severely rattled," as anyone might well be after such a tragedy. Such a request from Bernatchez makes sense in the light of the above explanation of his absence on that occasion. Otherwise, being the efficient officer that he was, he would surely have gone over to discover for himself what had gone wrong, and personally assessed the condition of the CO of the West Novas. And that is the nearest we will come to an explanation for the tragedy. It was one of those situations in which fate intervened, so that Bernatchez, brilliant tactician that he had proven himself to be in previous battles, was not present to guide the planning of a successful attack.

No fault can be found with the officers and men who carried out this ill-fated attempt. Their behaviour was exemplary. The attack leaders, Maj. Alan Nicholson and Capt. Stanley Smith, both of whom had been wounded in previous battles, had spent the summer absorbing reinforcements and training them for battle. Aware there were fatal flaws in the battle plan, they nonetheless obeyed orders, each probably realizing that it

Chapter Seven

would be his last action. They moved steadily forward until they and their men were cut down by mines, machine-gun fire, shells, and mortars. "Theirs is not to make reply, / Theirs is not to reason why, / Theirs is but to do and die," as Tennyson described the response of the trained soldier to a blunder in leadership during the Crimean War.

The stretcher-bearers and carrying parties displayed and exemplified the spirit of the true soldier in the face of disaster. As stretcher-bearer Alvin Hastings explained to me when he came to seek my assistance, "We do not carry arms and take no part in the fighting, which the others have to undertake. We are trained to render aid on the battlefield as and when needed, and they are calling for us now." There was no concern about what would happen to them as they went out to attempt the task—the men needed them now and they must respond. I went with them without delay. There is a passage in the New Testament in which Jesus says, "There is no greater love than this, that a man should lay down his life for his friends" (John 15:13). These young men were prepared to do just that without hesitation, like young Victor Newell, who lost his life as he searched for two missing comrades on the day after the battle.

Under normal circumstances this was no place for a chaplain, a fact that was pressed upon me a few days later in separate conversations with the CO and the brigadier. They pointed out that there was but one chaplain for each unit, and if I became a casualty there would be no one left to provide counselling, conduct burial services, write to next-of-kin, and strengthen the morale of the troops, among many other functions. Each impressed upon me his hope that I would, in future, remain with the regimental aid post during battle. I fully understood the logic of their counsel and I concurred with their request. It was not the first time I had had this pointed out to me. Why, then, had I gone out with the troops on what I knew was a most hazardous undertaking?

I had been apprehensive about a forthcoming action that I was convinced was going to devastate the lives of the young men with whom I had developed meaningful relationships. In my calling as chaplain I was committed to them as a counsellor and a friend. These men had attended the services I conducted on Sundays whenever possible, and many of them had also attended Wednesday-evening Bible discussion groups at which I helped them to understand the documents that are at the foundation of the Christian tradition. What was I to do under these very special circumstances?

One dimension of a chaplain's task with men engaged in war is to be a presence, to be visibly with them and concerned for them as they face life-threatening situations. Knowing the manner in which this particular assignment was laid on, it would have been impossible for me to have rested, let alone sleep, realizing the tragedy awaiting them. The least I could do was accompany them and go as far as possible, and to be of assistance as opportunity offered.

We held a burial service at 1700 hours on Friday, September 1, and laid to rest the bodies of thirteen of our comrades killed on the battlefield on August 31. I spent the evening sorting and forwarding their personal effects to brigade. Many years later, when I was privileged to visit the cemeteries in the area, I learned that eleven of the wounded we had carried out had died a few days later in field hospitals. They at least knew that their comrades had done everything possible to save them.

On the edge!

Chapter Eight

Fierce Fighting and Close Calls
September 1944
Foglia River / Cattolica / San Fortunato

On the night of August 31–September 1, three lanes were cleared through the minefields to the left of the West Novas' attack area, and the Royal 22nd Regiment went through and captured Point 133, clearing the way for the armour to pour through and chase the retreating enemy to their prepared positions along the coastal road.

Those officers and senior NCOs who had been left out of battle came forward and commenced the process of reorganizing the two companies for battles ahead. On Saturday, September 2, after a night of poor sleep followed by a light breakfast, we were on our way again across the Foglia River and up through the enemy's strongpoints to enter the Gothic Line defences. We passed a number of reinforced concrete pillboxes of the type we had first seen at the Hitler Line, featuring Tiger tank turrets with a 360-degree traverse. One of those I personally examined had been placed in the ditch dug for it, and was well stocked with ammunition, but the ditch had not been filled in with earth and the gun had never been fired, indicating that we had arrived sooner than the enemy expected us.

We paused at noon and remained at the Gothic Line for the rest of the day. I spent the afternoon sorting, listing, packaging, and sending off to brigade the personal effects of those we had buried, and the evening reporting to War Graves Registration and attending to correspondence. Although I was physically exhausted at night I was unable to sleep. I lay awake most of the night reflecting upon the events of August 31. I was torn apart by the unnecessary waste of lives at the Foglia River disaster. I felt I was finished and had no more to give to the war effort, and I inwardly wished that the powers that be would pull me out before I fell apart entirely. But nothing happened. I do not suppose my superiors even realized what we had gone through, and I was left with the West Novas to sink or swim and would have to somehow adjust. How I would have benefited from just one day off to mourn my friends and companions whom I had buried in an Italian grave or helped to carry out to some hospital down the line. I had no more stomach for war and desperately wanted out, but I was not about to ask for that.

Somehow I carried on, opening myself up more and more to God as we moved into the attack on Rimini. The 1st Canadian Division had broken through the Gothic Line defences, but the war was not over and we still had some bloody fighting ahead. So I faced my task, withdrawing somewhat into myself, and always seeking longer periods to be alone with God. I prayed he might heal me internally and enable me to cope with the tasks ahead.

On Sunday, September 3, the fifth anniversary of the beginning of the war, I conducted services for the four rifle companies, consisting of prayer, thanksgiving, and rededication to the unfinished task. The theme and lesson for the service was taken from 8 Deuteronomy: "Thou shalt remember all the ways in which the Lord Thy God has led thee." On Monday afternoon we moved up to a point just below Cattolica, within sound of the guns, and while here the CO had a talk with me. Ronnie discussed my action during the crisis at the Foglia River crossing. He told me that he had recommended me for a decoration following my action in the Hitler Line battle, but the authorities had not granted it. He put my name in again for recognition of my leadership in evacuating the wounded on August 31, but he could not foretell what the response might be. He then urged me to remain at the regimental aid post during future action, pointing out for the third time the complications for the regiment should I become a casualty. I agreed that the battlefield was no place for a padre. I was there to help, to guide men to God, and could accomplish no purpose by going into battle and becoming a casualty.

During future battles I did remain at the regimental aid post as much as possible, to render such aid as necessary to the wounded as they came through. After the battles, I went up to attend to the burials with assistance from the Pioneers. I am sad to say that I was kept busy.

On Wednesday, September 6, we were billeted in a large house where I had a room on the third floor for the padre's office. For the first time in weeks I had privacy and could spend some time in reflection and prayer. There was much for which to thank God. Somehow his unseen hand had guided us through the minefield ordeal until the last man was carried out. I then prayed by name for all the officers and men who had been killed or wounded, and for their next-of-kin, and I prayed for the officers and men who must now continue the unfinished task and pursue it to a successful conclusion.

The Advance to Rimini, 3–22 September 1944

More men were now seeking personal counselling from me, and I was becoming a helpful resource to the MO. I attended to one young man who had been sent out by his company commander at Riccione because he suffered from claustrophobia. Whenever he heard a shell coming, he would jump out of his slit trench and run for the nearest building or other shelter, and he was thus considered a liability to the men in his platoon. The MO could not send him back as suffering from battle fatigue, so he passed him on to me. We met in my third-floor office. The man was shaking, uncoordinated, and guilty about his behaviour. I encouraged him to talk about himself and he did so very forthrightly. He told me of his childhood and youth and then he gave me an account of his most unsatisfactory military experience with the regiment in action.

I listened attentively and then I told him that his real problem was a fear of being hit by a shell and dying, and that his fear of dying was related to his fear of God. From what he told me I gathered he was a believer, but that his idea of the Almighty was of a judgemental and vengeful God. I suggested that he look in the New Testament, when Jesus discloses that God is love and is personally concerned for our welfare. I assured him that I had experienced the same fears of dying, but that God was with us to help us and to save us. I suggested that, if he put his faith in Christ, he would be renewed inwardly and not be afraid to die.

I suggested that we ask for God's help, so we knelt and prayed. As we got up, he said: "I'm going back to my company. I'm all right now." Remarkably, his shaking had gone. I advised him to wait a few hours until the shelling died down, but he was resolved to go without delay, and, putting on his gear, he went off, to the great surprise of the MO. Halfway through the week he sent a message to me with a wounded man whom he had assisted off the battlefield: "Tell the padre I am still going strong. I tremble like a leaf every time a shell comes over, but I'm staying in my slit trench and doing my job." Three days later he came through as a walking wounded casualty, having been shot through the arm. This chap was quite transformed, fully in charge of himself and measuring up well as a member of his platoon. He was, in every sense, a new man in Christ.

It was with great difficulty that I remained at the regimental aid post during the three-day battle for San Lorenzo in Corregiano, near Rimini, and I was greatly relieved when the CO laid on a burial party for me to direct. I went up with the quartermaster to meet an appointed digging party under Cpl. Alton MacDonald. We needed a large plot, so we selected a piece of ground at the west end of a large stone barn about a mile south of San Lorenzo. Corporal Rafuse marked off the area into rows of graves and the men started digging. I commenced the sad task of searching the pockets of the dead as they were brought in, removing their identity tags, then sorting, listing, and wrapping their personal effects. The parcels were then sent to Brigade for forwarding to next-of-kin.

A major east-west road ran just north of the barn, and as we were working a squadron of British tanks came rumbling down it on their way to the forward area. They immediately drew heavy shellfire. The digging parties were in danger, so I called them off, and the corporal and I led them around to a patio, covered by a stone and tile roof, on the south side of the barn where there was a wine cellar. I sent the digging parties into the wine cellar while I remained on the patio to work, using one small wine cask as a seat

Fierce Fighting and Close Calls

and a larger one as a table. Corporal MacDonald showed some concern about my being so exposed, saying that the day before five men had been wounded right where I was seated. I felt that the situation was different now that we had driven the enemy from San Lorenzo, but he insisted that it was too risky. I agreed to come into the wine cellar as soon as I finished my time-consuming job.

Just then a British three-ton truck, with the tarp up and loaded with ammunition, rolled into the yard and drew up to the patio for shelter from the shelling. Corporal MacDonald became more agitated and said he must see me right now. I put down my pen, slipped my little black book of records into my pocket, and stepped over to the door of the wine cellar. The corporal immediately grabbed my arm and pulled me away from the doorway. At that precise moment a shell came through the patio roof directly over the spot where I had been sitting, and exploded, sending tons of burning rubble from the roof onto the wine casks, which were crushed to pieces. The whole scene became an immense conflagration with exploding small arms ammunition from the burning truck in front of the patio.

We had only seconds before the larger shells would explode, so I led the group out through the burning rubble and into the main barn area. No sooner had we closed the heavy oak door than all hell broke loose with exploding shells and mortars. Corporal MacDonald had saved me from certain death. I wasn't wearing my beret and it was consumed in the fire along with my chaplain's badge and fountain pen, and all the parcels of personal effects on which I was working. A Princess Patricia's major who had sought shelter for his company in the barn, and now feared it might collapse, ordered us all out through a dung hole close to the floor on the north side. For the next half-hour we lay in shallow ditches alongside the road while that precious load of ammunition hurtled through the air like missiles. A three-inch mortar bomb came spinning over the barn and landed a few feet from me where I was trying to dig myself in with the butt end of a pair of scissors; fortunately, it did not explode.

There was no possibility of continuing our task while the situation remained so unsettled, so I rode back to the regimental aid post with the quartermaster, Cecil Whynacht. Cecil had the back seat of his jeep piled with equipment that had been retrieved by carrying parties who brought out the dead. There was one walking wounded man to be brought out, so I let him sit in the passenger seat beside Cecil while I perched on top of the pile of equipment. We had not gone far when an 88 mm shell struck a building behind us. We were at that moment rounding a curve at about forty miles per hour. A large piece of shrapnel or a spent tank shell, making an eerie fluttering sound, passed directly in front of my face, from right to left, and just behind Cecil's head. It was so close that I felt its heat on my face. I had a ringing in my right ear afterwards, while Cecil experienced a similar sensation in his left ear. We arrived at the regimental aid post without further incident. In the early evening I returned with the jeep and worked with the Pioneers to bury all our casualties that had been brought out from the companies.

I frequently reflect on that brush with death. It almost seemed as though some demonic agency had my number and was determined to eliminate me. But, as on other similar occasions, deliverance was at hand, on this occasion through the concern of the corporal who had made me move immediately, and, by the grace of God, saved my life. We learned later that the 1st Canadian Division had been sent forward as a spear thrust to capture the Rimini airfield and the enemy forces were behind us on both flanks. The enemy observation posts, therefore, had a clear view of the row of trucks against the south wall of the barn. These made excellent targets for their guns.

I learned many years later, in a book by Robert Dietz entitled *Oath of Allegiance,* that Dietz, a twenty-year-old officer cadet who had already been wounded three times, was acting as a forward observation officer with the German forces, and directing fire on our position at that time. His site was spotted and attacked by one of our aircraft, wounding and putting the observation post out of commission. Thus we were able to move about without interference from artillery from that source for the next few days.

The San Fortunato ridge ran east and west, about two miles beyond San Lorenzo, ending above the coastal town of Rimini. It was one of the strongest positions in the Gothic Line defences and the final bastion in the system. Through September 16 and 17, while I was gathering and burying the dead from the bitter fighting for San Lorenzo, the West Novas were busy reorganizing and being reinforced. Still, these reinforcements were insufficient for our needs in officers and men, and it became necessary to merge C and D Companies into one company under the command of Maj. Gordie MacNeil, who had recently returned to the regiment.

On the morning of Monday, September 18, I attended an orders group at tactical HQ with the MO. We learned that Colonel Waterman had been replaced as CO of the regiment by the second-in-command, Maj. Frank Hiltz. Frank, a Nova Scotian, had been posted to the West Novas as second in command shortly after Waterman became CO, which was just prior to my posting as chaplain. He had been running a variety of training programs at B Echelon and relieving the CO at times. Throughout those months he was among those left out of battle and holding himself in readiness to take charge should the CO be disabled. He was being given a brief period of leadership in the regiment as 3rd Brigade launched a major attack to capture the San Fortunato ridge.

While completing work on the cemetery, I learned that an Allied bomber had mistakenly bombed a church in San Lorenzo, in the basement of which a platoon of A Company along with one of Royal Canadian Engineers had their headquarters. The place had collapsed and buried them. Several of our men had been wounded, and I went up to assist in digging them out. We evacuated five of the Engineers, but three had died. In assisting to dig out one of their men who was completely covered with debris, the man pleaded with us to cut his leg off at the thigh, rather than continue digging. However, we dug him out, saved the leg, and evacuated him.

During this lull in the fighting, the Royal Canadian Regiment, Carleton and Yorks, and West Novas all shared one building for their regimental aid posts, the first time this had been possible. I spent the afternoon burying three of our men, three Engineers, and two Germans. I went to bed after supper suffering from a bad cold in my head and chest.

At 1900 hours Major Hiltz held an orders group at which the West Novas were ordered to attack and secure the hilltop village of San Fortunato. A and B Companies were assigned the first phase, starting from the Ausa River, which had been secured by the Carleton and Yorks. They went off at 0400 hours on Tuesday, September 19, and met sporadic small arms fire, but reached their objective, the lateral road at the base of the hill. As daylight dawned they were joined by two troops of tanks and launched the second phase of the attack, directly up the hill. The tanks were immediately engaged by the enemy firing on them from along the ridge above. Four of our tanks were knocked out. We learned later that one of the guns was on a Tiger tank stationed on the ground floor at the east end of a large hospital, a large red cross painted on its walls. The tank would move out to a doorway or window, fire at the tanks below, then retreat inside the hospital for cover while its officer picked out his next target. This was a brazen violation of international agreements. Our guns at no time fired upon the hospital.

The infantry pushed on with the attack, now unaccompanied by armour, and both the West Novas and the Hasty Ps got halfway up the hill. They held their ground despite merciless enemy fire throughout the day. A second assault by 2nd Brigade and 3rd Brigade was successful in driving the enemy from their strongholds, leaving behind several hundred prisoners, many of whom were found in the basement of the hospital. At the regimental aid post, which was now located west of San Lorenzo, we cared for the wounded, working steadily until 2100 hours.

September 20 was a relatively quiet day, with fewer casualties, so the MO and I went up to tactical HQ to arrange for the evacuation of the dead for burial in the plot below San Lorenzo. The regiment was still in action, although the fighting had ceased for the moment, and the men were exhausted. Lt. Col. A.L. Saunders, a former brigade major, took over the regiment at that time and his influence became immediately apparent. Casualties were brought in during the evening and more arrived by jeep at 0400 hours on Thursday, September 21, demonstrating the need for a designate jeep and driver to bring in our casualties from the forward area.

That Thursday I worked all morning and most of the afternoon at San Fortunato, wrapping up bodies in blankets for burial and checking the identity of personal effects and records for each. We prepared thirteen bodies for transport to the cemetery, to be laid to rest beside their comrades who had given their lives in the liberation of San Lorenzo. Ultimately, during the three weeks of battles at the Gothic Line the West Novas lost 330 killed and wounded, including twenty-one officers, and not a single platoon commander survived unscathed.

top left, Padre Wilmot seated high up in the Colosseum; top right, at a campsite in a vineyard; upper-middle left, West Nova men who were confirmed by the Bishop of Lichfield at All Saints Anglican Cathedral, Rome; upper-middle right, West Nova officers and a casualty; lower-middle left, a tank concealed in a ruined house; bottom left, the Mortar Platoon of the WNSR at a front-line open-air shower stall; bottom right, West Nova Scotia Regiment cemetery, near San Lorenzo.

top left, a German tank taken by the West Novas in the Lamone Advance; top right, Lt. Col. A.L. Saunders; middle left, Padre Wilmot with his truck; top middle right, Col. J.L. Ralston visiting the regiment after the battle at the Gothic Line; bottom right, dedication of the WSNR cemetery at Russi; bottom left, Padre Wilmot giving the blessing at a farewell service.

CHAPTER NINE

A Time of Stress and a Moment of Rest
September – November 1944
Cattolica / Rome / Savignano / Cesena

We returned to Cattolica for much-needed rest, to regroup, and, hopefully, to bring the platoons up to strength with reinforcements. On Sunday, September 24, I held a battalion parade service. The lesson was from Isaiah 40: 25–31, in which the unknown prophet of the exile, designated by scholars the Deutero-Isaiah, begins his message of encouragement and promise of renewal for the Jews enduring exile in Babylon. In my address to these men, who were exhausted and somewhat disillusioned, I spoke on the need to seek inward renewal.

My reading for the day was Psalm 8, which asks the question: "What is man?" A most important question to ask at a time when human lives were being eliminated so abruptly.

On Monday, September 25, the new CO, Lt. Col. Al Saunders, held an orders group to introduce himself to the officers of the regiment, followed by a meeting of the company commanders. In the evening the officers held a mess dinner to say farewell to Colonel Waterman, who had been CO of the West Novas since December 1943, when Colonel Bogert was wounded and he, as second-in-command, took over. It was sad to see him go. He was the most colourful and dynamic leader the regiment had had during my time with them, and at times his leadership had been brilliant. Whether or not he had been entirely responsible for the debacle at the Foglia River crossing will never be known, but he, as commanding officer, had to accept the responsibility and pay the price for failure.

That evening I had a long chat with Brigadier Bernatchez, who wanted to hear about my experiences at the Foglia River on August 31, particularly our removal of the wounded from the minefield, and Victor Newell's death the following day. The brigadier expressed surprise that we had returned to a live minefield, but I explained that the CO had asked us to search for two missing men and that we had done so with his assurance that the area had been swept. Brigadier Bernatchez emphasized throughout our conversation that one should never risk the lives of the living to remove the dead, who should be removed only after all danger to life has been cleared. I fully concurred, but stressed that Newell and I had been searching for two men who might have been alive but wounded. I also remarked on the inadequacy of sweeping techniques and the special difficulties in detecting Schu mines, which contain little, if any, metal.

On Thursday afternoon we toured the eleventh-century Castle Gradara located on a promontory just south of Cattolica. The castle was well preserved, complete with the instruments of torture used throughout the Inquisition. Victims would be tortured until they renounced their heresy and confessed the truth, at which time they would be dispatched down a chute to the bottom of the cliff. A special doorway revealed stairs that led down from the living quarters to permit the women to descend and watch the process from a balcony. Beside the doorway hung a beautiful painting of the Virgin and Child, reminding the spectators that the torture they were about to witness was being carried out to turn the victim to Christ. As Alfred North Whitehead remarked in reviewing this period of European history, "the Medieval world was populated with terrified Christians."

On Friday afternoon we were visited by Col. J. Layton Ralston, Minister of National Defence in the Mackenzie King government. Colonel Ralston met with the officers, the brigadier introducing me as the padre who had got several holes in his helmet. In speaking with us he remarked that as an old soldier he could readily observe that the battalion was sadly under-reinforced. He promised to get more reinforcements over without delay, adding that, if he failed, he would tender his resignation as minister. Prime Minister Mackenzie King had received a strong vote from the people of Canada to conscript men for overseas duty, but he had resisted doing so for fear of losing support in Quebec. He refused Ralston's plea for more men and Ralston resigned his office. So the regiment went into its next action very much under strength.

Sunday, October 1, was a clear but windy day, and the brigade service was held outside. The Scripture reading for the service was Luke 14:25: "Whosoever forsaketh not all that he hath cannot be my disciple." In the sermon I emphasized the three prerequisites for battle: renunciation, mastery of fear, and vision of the task, that is, to recognize that our end goal was the defeat of tyranny.

In the afternoon, learning of possible action in the near future, I went to see Colonel Saunders to inquire whether I should remain. He insisted that visits to the men were important and that I should proceed forward as planned.

We set out early on Monday morning for Jesi, where I visited patients in hospital, and in the afternoon we drove through the deep gorges of the Apennines to Perugia where I spent Tuesday at No. 14 Canadian General Hospital visiting patients. On Wednesday we called at Assisi, where I visited Lieutenant Embree and Capt. Pat Bates in hospital. I had originally met Pat Bates at Halifax when we were both serving in the Black Watch. He reappeared during the attack on San Fortunato ridge, having been rushed forward to take over a platoon of West Novas without any prior preparation, and there he was wounded.

Pressing on, we arrived at Rome in the late afternoon and I spent the evening at No. 5 Canadian General Hospital tracking down eight of our men. I set out for Caserta early Friday morning, October 6, and stayed there for two days. While there I had lunch with Maj. Alan Nicholson and Lieutenants Craig and McPhee, all three of whom were casualties from the Foglia River tragedy. It was refreshing to see them recovering from their wounds, for they were in bad shape when we carried them out.

On my return journey from this round of hospital visits I stopped for two days' relaxation in Rome, as recommended by Colonel Saunders. I treated myself to a Turkish bath and a massage, and spent an afternoon viewing European paintings from past centuries. One evening I pursued my interest in opera, attending Verdi's *La Forza del Destino*. I revisited the Church of St. John Lateran and I also climbed the monument of Garibaldi.

On Friday, October 13, after my return to Cattolica, the Bishop of Portsmouth came to Riccione for Confirmation, which was attended by all the Corps chaplains, a padre from the New Zealand forces, and the senior chaplain of the 8th Army. After lunch, the senior chaplain spoke to us of the great shortage of chaplains in the British Army at this juncture, casualties having been very heavy. The British and Canadian chaplains discussed the possibility of parish exchanges following the war, though nothing came of it.

On Saturday I spoke with Private Osborne, now recovered from his wounds and back with his company, who called to tell me that he was going strong and able to do his job. I also met with Pte. Alvin Hastings, who had displayed tremendous courage and calmness in working with the wounded throughout the Foglia River tragedy and the battles for San Lorenzo and the San Fortunato ridge, and who was in need of a rest or a change of role. He became my batman driver.

On Wednesday, October 18, we left our peaceful life at Cattolica. I bade goodbye to my truck, and travelled with the regimental aid post, moving up to Savignano to relieve the 48th Highlanders. On Thursday morning I visited C Company and remained with them for lunch. Earlier that morning they had occupied a large house that had been a bishop's palace. On checking, they discovered a deep basement with two beds already made up and a thick rug covering the floor. Suspecting that something was amiss, they examined the room carefully. Under the rug they found a trap door in the floor and could clearly hear a clock ticking. On opening the door they discovered a ton or more of dynamite, all set to go off at noon to blow up the house and all its occupants. They pulled the fuse and removed the dynamite. We would all have be blown sky high had it not been discovered.

After lunch the regimental aid post moved north onto the main Bologna road. The following day Colonel Saunders called at the regimental aid post at breakfast time and invited me to visit B and C Companies with him. Apples and pears were plentiful in B Company area, hanging ripe from the trees, but before picking them we had to be careful they were not booby-trapped with mines. We visited C Company in the bishop's palace, which had been completely looted and ransacked by the enemy. They had slashed beautiful paintings with their bayonets and thrown the contents of cupboards and drawers outside in a pile. I picked up a few souvenirs from the debris—a silver tablespoon with a bishop's crest on it, a small brass bell, a tiny coloured vase, and a few glass stones that had at one time belonged to a necklace.

The front had moved on and Cesena was entirely in our hands. Before we moved there on Saturday, October 21, I buried two Germans found dead in a field near the regimental aid post. Both wore symbols of the Roman Catholic faith about their necks. Over the next few days at Cesena, 2 Brigade, on our right, let loose a heavy artillery barrage that Jerry countered with mortars and heavy shells. Several shells landed near our building and one struck the balcony of the building next to us, but there were no direct hits. We were at that time attached to 2 Brigade, which sought to establish a bridgehead over the Savio River. A and D Companies had both attempted to cross the river, only to be driven back by tanks. Two of our men were wounded and we also received two enemy casualties, one of whom wore a crucifix. He was just a boy, too young even to shave. The other one was badly wounded. He took his wedding ring out of his small wallet, put it on his finger, joined his hands together, closed his eyes, and offered a prayer. He had lost a lot of blood but his breathing was strong and he was conscious when he left.

Saturday, October 28, was a day full of frustrations. In the past few weeks the regiment had been commanded by two untried officers and morale had quickly waned. We had also received a new medical officer. Standard routines and procedures were being neglected, and petty thievery had become common in the regimental aid post. I felt so disgusted with all the double-crossing going on amongst the ranks that in the evening I had a talk with the CO. We discussed the problems further when he took me with him on a reconnaissance to select the best route for our forthcoming move to Cattolica.

On Sunday I rode to Cattolica in a jeep, arriving at noon to find good billets and a fine office for the padre. I spoke to our new MO again and pointed out that he was in charge of the regimental aid post, not the sergeant who was taking advantage of the situation. The sergeant's task was to see that the regimental aid post staff carried out the MO's instructions. I also had a heart-to-heart talk with the regimental aid post sergeant about the disappearance of my excellent brass primus stove, which I had purchased at Pompeii in the summer and upon which my batman depended to get our meals. To my great surprise, the primus was returned half an hour after my talk with the sergeant. From that point on I had the full co-operation of all in the regimental aid post.

Tuesday, October 31, was my elder daughter's tenth birthday, and I observed a longer than usual period in prayer. I prayed for my wife and children and all my relations. I prayed for myself, that I might be true in character, and for the officers and men of the regiment who were discussing their problems openly with me, particularly the disintegration of morale from so many changes in leadership. I prayed about a planned visit with the Senior Chaplain, my preparations for forthcoming Padre's Hours, and for the planned enrichment of Sunday programs while in reserve.

On Thursday afternoon, November 2, I held a Padre's Hour on the subject of belief in God. I gave a prepared talk in which I touched on the wide variety of beliefs that people hold, and at its conclusion I invited anyone with different views to express them. Corporal Johnson spoke up and said that he had been through about as much flak from the enemy as anyone in the regiment and that he had found no reason to change his convictions as an atheist. I thanked him for his contribution to the discussion and invited others to speak from their personal experience. There followed a lively discussion on the reality of religion from several of the fighting men. As the men left the hall, I thanked Corporal Johnson again for his participation and invited him to come to my office for further discussion. I learned later that he was reprimanded by his officer, who threatened to put him on charge for speaking as he did. I am pleased to report that he did come and see me a couple of weeks later as I was about to leave for a mess dinner. I cancelled the dinner and enjoyed a valuable discussion in which he shared his thoughts with me and explained how he had come to hold his present convictions. I loaned him one of C.S. Lewis's books, which we later discussed.

On Sunday afternoon I had an interview with one Alex Vingar. This young man had demonstrated outstanding courage in leadership. In the heat of battle at the Hitler Line he assisted in the release of a platoon that had been taken prisoner and was in the process of being marched off by the enemy—an action for which he was awarded the Military Medal. But after the battle the poor man learned that his marriage had broken up and he went to pieces, going AWOL for a time before returning to the regiment. Sergeant Vingar was received back, minus his stripes, as Private Vingar. Such was his rank until his death from shellfire during the taking of Russi in December.

Another man came in on Monday. He had received word the night before from his brother-in-law that his wife was living with another man. Could he possibly get back to Canada? I promised to see the adjutant and did so at noon. I also had a talk with him about the real problem and its solution in Christ. My diary states that he was appreciative, that he knelt in prayer and put his trust in Christ. I gave him a New Testament and encouraged him to read it daily and to ask God to disclose himself to him. These men had been too long away from their families and their morale went to pieces on learning that their home lives had disintegrated.

CHAPTER TEN

Roman Holiday, Russi Road
November – December 1944
Rome / Russi / Cattolica

Knowing that I had some leave coming up, I prepared by reading travel literature. Early in August I had spent forty-eight hours on the south bank of the Arno, overlooking Florence, and I was thrilled with the thought of actually being able to walk across the Ponte Vecchio and visit the famous Duomo. So on Friday, November 17, I set out from Cattolica at 0900 hours for Florence, my driver, Dennis, at the wheel of my truck.

We drove to Jesi, where we stopped for lunch with some Italian friends of Dennis, then drove on into the Apennines on roads blanketed with fresh snow. Our truck broke down just south of Fabriano, necessitating an overnight stay while the vehicle was towed away for repairs. We were told that a new clutch box was needed and it would take at least a day to fix. So, time being of the essence on army leave, I took the first ride that was offered—a leave-truck bound for Rome—and was delivered to the Officer's Club Hotel in time for supper. I had been to Rome briefly on three previous occasions and had also read much about the Eternal City, so I had a good idea of what I wanted to see during the next few days in that ancient centre of civilization.

After breakfast on Sunday, I set forth with Stewart East, padre of the 48th Highlanders, to visit St. Peter's and attend High Mass. We then went to All Saints Anglican Church in the centre of the city for Morning Prayer and Holy Communion. In the afternoon we visited the catacombs of St. Calixtus; these great underground passageways were first used as cemeteries by the early Christians and later as meeting places in times of persecution. Walking along the passageways and scrutinizing the Greek inscriptions on the walls, we had the feeling that we were treading upon holy ground.

On emerging from the catacombs, we walked to some caves where, it had just been discovered, the Germans had massacred 335 prominent

Chapter Ten

Italian citizens in reprisal for an attempt made on the life of a general on March 24. It was poignant to walk among the sorrowing people as they viewed the hundreds of caskets. If any proof were needed of the horrors that would have been visited upon leaders of the Western world had the Nazis conquered, it was plainly laid out before us.

We then visited the Church of San Sebastian and the Colosseum, from where we went on to the Basilica di San Pietro in Vincoli (St. Peter in Chains). It is named thus because it was originally built to hold the chains with which King Herod had bound Peter in Jerusalem, as recorded in Acts 12:1–13. We also paused to admire Michelangelo's famous sculpture of Moses.

That evening after an early supper, I was fortunate to be able to continue my education in opera by seeing a performance of Verdi's *La Traviata*.

Over the next few days Stewart and I crammed in as much sightseeing as possible. We visited some of my favourite places from previous sojourns in Rome, such as the Forum and the Vatican, and explored unfamiliar attractions like the majestic Basilica di San Paolo Fuori le Mura (St. Paul without the Walls). On Tuesday and Wednesday we were accompanied by a knowledgeable guide, which made for a considerably more educational tour. On Wednesday afternoon I enjoyed another operatic performance, this time Mascagni's *Cavalleria Rusticana*.

On Thursday, November 23, my leave over, I packed my bags and checked out of the hotel in the morning. I visited No. 5 Canadian General Hospital until 1400 hours, when Dennis and I set out for home. We stopped to dine with Dennis's Italian friends at Jesi and arrived back at Cattolica at 0200 hours on Friday.

My leave in Rome was the most refreshing break I had during the two years that I served overseas. After months of bloody fighting, from the Foglia River crossing through to the battles for Rimini, I was exhausted and somewhat disillusioned and needed an opportunity to pull back and take a long look at the situation. This I found in my tours of Rome and its ancient ruins. In fact, the week in Rome provided vivid reminders of the roots of that civilization in defence of which men were laying down their lives. Scene after scene reminded us of our Judeo-Christian heritage, of the rich history of Greek thought, and of the genius for organization of the Roman Empire with its centuries of the Pax Romana, which had permitted the spread of Christianity throughout Europe, and hence to Britain.

I returned from my leave convinced and reassured that the faith which had survived centuries of turmoil and had brought order to the Western world would weather this storm, including the confusion that we all realized would face the world after the end of hostilities. With continued ded-

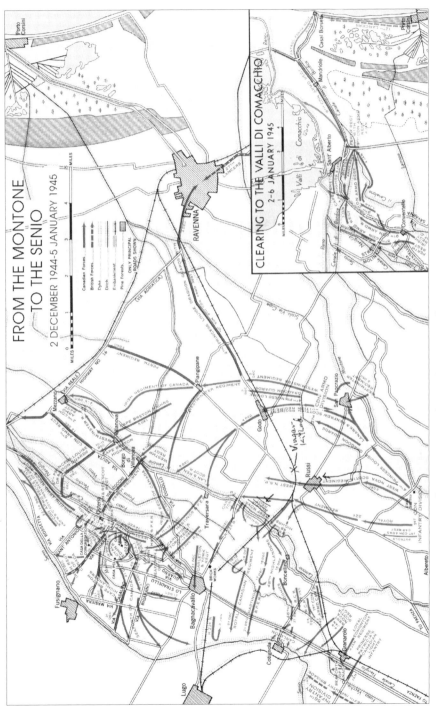

From the Montone to the Senio, 2 December 1944–5 January 1945

ication to the task the enemy would finally be overthrown, and I turned my attention to that aspect of the task with renewed vigour.

The war claimed my full attention soon after my leave, with a new offensive. We moved out onto the Lombard Plain where we faced a new type of obstacle in the succession of rivers flowing down from the mountains with forty-foot dikes to contain the resulting flood waters, added to which were irrigation ditches, each with dikes that had to be scaled. Our first objective was the Russi canal, and the attack went in early on the morning of December 2, with B and C Companies leading. I went out with Private Hamper, driver of the regimental aid post carrier ambulance, to bring in some casualties, but we had great difficulty reaching them, the shellfire being particularly heavy. Hamper was an experienced driver and for the most part drove down the ditches to keep out of sight of enemy observation posts. When we arrived at the south side of the canal, I had him park the carrier ambulance behind a stone wall as a safeguard against shelling, while I went down the ditch to a house near the ruins of a bridge. The enemy had reduced the house to rubble, but two rooms in the basement were intact and were serving as B Company headquarters. Here I located the company commander, Maj. Harvey Jones, and his instrument man, sitting under a large oak table with a map of the area spread out, directing the attack.

They had lost contact with the platoons, which had crossed the canal and were being heavily shelled. As I arrived, a young runner emerged from the canal with a message giving directions for artillery fire on tanks and enemy strongpoints. I watched while the major called down artillery fire upon the attacking forces and drafted a message to send back to his platoon commanders. He then turned to the young runner, who was soaking wet and obviously cold, and said: "I think I had better send someone else back with this and send you out; you look exhausted." But the boy replied, "Oh no, sir, I can't leave them. Besides, I know the way back, having come across the canal once, and I must go back to my platoon. They will have dry clothes for me." And back he went across the canal to join his comrades in holding the position. The artillery stonk was successful. B Company held onto their bridgehead, and A and D Companies later crossed over to strengthen the position while the Engineers threw a Bailey bridge across and they were joined by our tanks to push on with the attack on Russi.

Meanwhile, once Major Jones was free for conversation, I discovered that the casualties we were seeking were not at B Company, so I returned to the carrier ambulance and went back to the regimental aid post. By early morning all our companies were across the canal and passing up through Russi. C Company, on the right, had a difficult time and suffered several casualties by shellfire. At this point the regimental aid post also crossed the canal and set up on the outskirts of the town of Russi. B Company passed through Russi and the platoons took up positions south of the railway track with D Company on the right. They attacked the railway track and took it, but were driven back by enemy tanks and machine-gun fire. As our tanks came up to give support they passed by D Company headquarters and were heavily mortared. Captain Drewery, the artillery forward observation officer, Major Rhodes, the officer commanding D Company, and Lt. Don Campbell were all wounded, as were others.

It was just north of the railway tracks that Pte. Alex Vingar received his mortal wound. It was obvious that he was badly injured and, at the request of Walter Garber, acting company commander, I went out with the regimental aid post jeep ambulance and stretcher-bearer to bring him in, only to discover that the shell had blown off his right leg and buttock. While the driver was turning the jeep around, I realized that he was dead; in fact, rigor mortis had already set in. I then recalled the brigadier's warning not to risk the lives of the living to bring out the dead, and at the same moment I realized the enemy had this spot pinpointed for their mortars. On my command, we tossed the stretcher back on the jeep and jumped in. Just as the jeep lurched forward, there was a terrific crash as the mortars started to fall, throwing debris and dirt all over the jeep, but no shrapnel hit us. The first mortar landed where the jeep had been one second earlier. Had I not responded immediately, we would have become casualties. I thanked God for Brigadier Bernatchez's forthright counsel.

The attack proceeded successfully throughout the night. I did not get to bed at all, but went out at 0200 hours to see the men of D Company as they were setting out on the next leg of their attack. I also assisted in bringing in Corporal Miller, who had been reported killed but was found to be still alive. The regimental aid post did a marvellous job of resuscitating him and sent him on to the car post, to be picked up and taken to the casualty clearing station.

For the next two days I was busy gathering up our dead from the battlefield and burying them in a battalion cemetery that we had laid out in an apple orchard just south of Russi. This task was distressing me more and more, since many of the dead were men with whom I had worked for the best part of a year. Vingar, for example, had gone through the Hitler Line battles, where he had distinguished himself and been awarded the Military Medal. After he was buried we found his severed leg and buttock at a spot several yards' distance from where he was killed. We opened his grave and buried the limb beside his body. Here was but one of the many who had fought bravely in the face of personal family disintegration resulting from his long absence from home. At this point the ghastly contradictions of war were wearing me down.

Chapter Ten

After breakfast on Wednesday, December 6, I went down to tactical HQ to inquire about the need for further burials. There I learned that Maj. Harvey Jones, whose leadership had been vital to our success at the Russi canals, was dead from a shrapnel wound to his heart. His funeral service was held that morning at 1000 hours.

It was Jones's company that took the Russi canal crossing and held the bridgehead despite repeated and fierce counterattacks by the enemy, allowing the Engineers enough time to lay down a Bailey bridge, over which tanks and armour rolled to capture Russi. Although Jones's death was caused by shrapnel, it was generally agreed that exhaustion played a role, as he had been on the go for days without rest and didn't exercise his usual caution against stray shells. Throughout these weeks the Canadian Army had been seriously undermanned from lack of reinforcements, and under these conditions even the best men with the most experience are lost.

Colonel Saunders held an orders group to announce plans for an attack across the Lamone River and tactical HQ moved into a palazzo at the edge of the canal at the site for the West Novas' crossing. Due to daily changes in the flood levels, the attack had to be postponed on three successive days. During the wait we were heavily mortared on all sides, but the palazzo was strongly built and the mortars had no effect on it. On Friday, December 8, realizing the attack was postponed yet again, I went down to the main battalion to examine a motorcycle that had been "liberated" during the battle for the town of Russi. Someone thought it might help me to move more freely about the regiment. It had been sent to main battalion to be checked, where it was found that the vehicle needed more repairs than could be provided, so I arranged to have it sold and the proceeds placed in a cigarette fund for the men. I was actually relieved, for I personally felt much safer moving about on my two feet and able to take cover readily when necessary.

I arrived back at tactical HQ to find that Major Hart from brigade had come up to see me and to present to me a small silk ribbon—white with a mauve bar across it—the Military Cross. I sewed it on my battledress with my own hand. The Military Cross was awarded for my leadership and action in evacuating the wounded from the minefield during the intense battle at the Foglia River crossing, where the West Novas had attempted to break through the main defences of the Gothic Line. The award could not have come at a more opportune time, for my spirits were particularly low, and I was very near the point of physical exhaustion. I had supper that evening with C Company, on the invitation of Majors McNeil and McAdam, and received congratulations all throughout the evening.

Realizing there was going to be no movement over the weekend, I planned a number of services, particularly for the rifle companies. On Saturday I held services for A, B, and C Companies. In the afternoon I called at D Company to conduct a service for them, but they were being shelled very heavily and the company commander wisely decided not to assemble the men in one place under those conditions. Just before I arrived they had taken a direct hit on the far end of the large barn they were occupying. It came right through the roof and loft to the ground floor, where it exploded and killed a couple of cows. A family living in the next stall, having been displaced from their home, were badly shaken up, but no one was hurt. They later moved out. I postponed the service to the following day.

Sunday, December 10, was a beautiful day, but cold. I held services for HQ and Support Companies as well as D Company. I remained with D Company for lunch, a delicious steak dinner courtesy of the cow that had been killed by shellfire the day before. The CO held an orders group at 1600 hours, at which he announced that the attack on the Lamone River would commence that evening, following three devastating barrages.

The West Novas attacked on the north side of the railway bridge, with tactical HQ and the regimental aid post located in the large palazzo. We waited until after the third barrage and then rushed in with our two jeeps. Biggy's jeep was crowded off the road and slid into the ditch on its side, so we all climbed onto the field ambulance jeep and rode into the palazzo just in time to escape the enemy counter-barrage, which came down all around the castle and up the road.

C Company were caught in the enemy barrage and their carrying party with the pontoon bridge was decimated. A Company's bridge, too short for the swollen river, failed to reach the far shore and swung around in the current, so they were also unable to make the crossing. The 48th Highlanders on our left and the Carleton and Yorks on our right successfully crossed while we were under heavy shelling. Our D Company finally followed the 48th Highlanders' crossing on the railway bridge and closed in on our positions from the left; A and B Companies went through the Carleton and Yorks' crossing and closed in from the right on their objectives, salvaging what had all the appearance of a disaster. Our tank hunters knocked out two tanks and two SP guns, and by morning the positions were well held. Colonel Saunders forbade me to go out to bring in casualties, so Jack Garland, my batman, worked with Biggy all night. He had earlier been assigned to me as a batman assistant, to work with me while we were in action and ensure that I had a companion with me at all times in the event of injury. On this occasion Jack took on the task that I had been prevented from tackling, and he and the jeep driver worked throughout the night to bring in casualties. By morning our forces were all across the river and the enemy were falling back in front of Bagnacavalo.

Sgt. Alton MacDonald was killed by a mine while crossing the river on the railway bridge and embankment. This was the man who, as a corporal,

Chapter Ten

had been in charge of the burial party that laid out our cemetery just south of San Lorenzo, and who had saved my life from a direct hit on the roof under which I had been sitting. And now he was dead. He was found to be wearing a rosary about his neck and was reported to me as having been a member of the Roman Catholic Church, so I called Chaplain Hooper, of Brigade, who went up to conduct the funeral. But as Captain Hooper was preparing him for burial, he detached one of the two tags every man wore about his neck in those days, and discovered that he was not a Roman Catholic after all, but a member of the Presbyterian Church. Captain Hooper proceeded with the burial, but reported to me that MacDonald had belonged to my flock. I learned later that the sergeant's fiancée was a Roman Catholic and had sent him the rosary, so perhaps he received the last rites that, given a choice, he would have selected for himself.

As our front had moved forward, I spent the next several days gathering up and burying our dead in our regimental cemetery just south of Russi. Shelling was particularly heavy as the enemy continued to retreat under intense pressure from our forces, and by Thursday, December 21, they had moved back to the banks of the Senio River. I spent the day picking up the dead, which had been impossible to do until the positions were cleared, gathering three in the area north of Bagnacavalo and one in our former area south of the city. We buried them in our cemetery at Russi.

By the time we had completed this task it was quite dark. Being in the forward area, we had to drive without lights. As we were proceeding along the west side of the large dike that prevents the Lamone River from overflowing in rainy seasons, an anti-tank corps jeep proceeding south ran into us head-on. The visibility was very poor, but, fortunately for us, our driver was experienced and had his windshield down. He saw the approaching jeep coming straight at us on the wrong side of the road and stopped. The driver of the southbound jeep hit us at full speed causing both vehicles to rear up. There were three of us in the front seat. Sitting on the outside, I was crowded out, and I landed in the ditch on my head and shoulders, with one foot caught under the dash of the jeep. I was shaken but unhurt, since we had stopped before the collision occurred. Our grave-digging crew were in a small trailer behind our jeep and were also unhurt, but both driver and passenger in the other jeep required medical attention. Both jeeps were wrecks. We telephoned tactical HQ and Lieutenant Embree drove down and picked us up. It was good to get home in one piece.

We moved back from the forward area early in the morning of Saturday, December 23, to a rest area just north of Russi on the Russi–Ravenna highway, where the regimental aid post occupied a house opposite tactical HQ. I went with the MO to main battalion where Colonel Saunders informed us that he was no longer commanding officer of the West Novas. The regiment had failed to accomplish all that had been expected of it at the Lamone River crossing and someone must be held responsible, despite the fact that the men could not have done better under different leadership given the situation they faced. Someone must pay for mistakes, and those higher up never consider that it might have been their mistake in asking the impossible. So, we had a new commanding officer, Maj. Frank Hiltz.

I had a long talk with Colonel Saunders. He took the situation calmly and philosophically, knowing that he had done his best under the circumstances. He then informed me that he had recommended that I be transferred to a field ambulance unit or casualty clearing station after this action, so I must not be surprised should a change occur. Colonel Saunders felt that I had served long enough in actual battle conditions and should now go where my experience would be of value in ministering to men. This change would make way for someone else to come and experience the opportunities and dangers of service in a line regiment.

On Christmas Eve I held two services, after which there was carol singing in the regimental aid post for an hour or more. I then had a visit from Maj. John Cameron and Capt. Don Rice who both felt badly about recent changes in the leadership of the regiment. They were but two of a number of senior officers who felt that the commanding officer should have been appointed from among the senior officers who had served through many months of bitter fighting, and several of whom were legends and would have had the full confidence of the men. Instead, they once again had a commanding officer who had never led men in battle, not even as a platoon or company commander, and they realized that the morale of the regiment was suffering. Unfortunately, there was nothing that they or I could do about this and, as loyal officers of His Majesty's Service, they accepted the situation and supported the leaders they were given. After they had left I prayed at length for the regiment and its problems, including its new CO, Maj. Frank Hiltz who, as second-in-command for the past year, had been prevented from gaining any practical experience of leadership in battle while waiting in the wings to be available if and when called to take over.

At 0900 hours on December 25, I held a Christmas service for the rifle companies. Realizing that the men were all weary of the pattern of their wartime life, I prepared a special Christmas message, in which I likened our own unhappy circumstances to the awful conditions attending Christ's birth in a stable. I then drove down to Russi for two more services.

I said grace for the men of the rifle companies at their special Christmas dinner, then returned to the regimental aid post, where we all sat down to a delicious meal of turkey with all the trimmings, cake, and candy, and a bottle of beer for each man. Capt. Hyman Mendelson, who had served with us as MO through the Hitler and Gothic Line battles, came up to wish us a Merry Christmas, and I took him to visit the men in their company locations, returning at 1700 hours. I had supper at battalion HQ, and later had a long talk with Maj. Frank Hiltz, our new commanding officer. I finally got to bed at 0130 hours.

Chapter Eleven

Prayers for the Fallen

December 1944 – February 1945

Russi / Bagnacavalo

Our Christmas break was very brief, and by December 27 we were on the move again to relieve the 48th Highlanders south of Bagnacavalo. I visited B Company, tactical HQ and C Company and had lunch with a section of 13 Platoon. The men were billeted in houses and cow stables, the latter being much warmer than the houses. They seemed to be settling down under their new leadership and were feeling more rested. Patrols went out from three companies and all met the enemy in force. They retired with three casualties, all slightly wounded. Capt. Max Forsyth-Smith received a shrapnel wound in the thigh.

I found the lack of privacy in my living accommodation at that time very trying, providing no opportunity to be alone for prayer and meditation. Without prayer I did not feel ready for the day, to face the shells and flak. My only confidence was in God, and unless I kept in touch with him, I was easily frightened. Once assured of his presence I went out unafraid to wherever he led me, confident that, if it was his will, I should come through. My reading for the day was Matthew 6:19: "Store up no treasures for yourself on earth." My only treasures on earth were the love and devotion of my wife and children. These were treasures above all else given to me by God. My daily prayer was this: "I give these back to Thee, O God, for they are thine and we are thine. Our times are in Thy hand to lead us onward in Thy will for us. Amen."

On Friday, December 29, I visited the men of D Company and then went on to A Company, whose platoons were spread out, living in barns and houses on the north side of the canal. My batman, Jack Garland, and I made our way behind a low dike on the north side of the canal that also served as a dirt road, and then followed a footpath beside the water to keep out of sight of the enemy as much as possible. We experienced no difficulties until we left A Company HQ to return to D Company. We had followed the ditch on the way out until we were directly behind the large barn that housed the men, then we walked across a rough frozen muddy terrain to the barn. The platoon officer said this was unnecessary and on our way back directed us around the mud.

The enemy may have spotted us as we left the barn, but they waited until we were in an open space. An enemy artillery stonk of half a dozen shells landed on top of the dike and shrapnel sprayed into the water and the far bank, just skimming over our heads as we lay at the edge of the canal. They were deadly accurate, and if it had not been for the low dike we would have had it. Between stonks we crawled beside the water and wasted no time in getting into the shelter of No. 16 Platoon once we were opposite their building. We then went on to B Company HQ, and caught a ride to tactical HQ with Major Hiltz, who was on his way there. I was particularly glad to have had Jack with me on this occasion and appreciated the wisdom of the CO in providing someone to go with me at all times.

On Sunday, December 31, our men being spread out along the canal, I held a service for Protestant personnel at Brigade at 1000 hours. I spoke on the twofold message of the day, "God with us" and our daily need for God's Spirit to help us be our true selves in the year before us. After lunch I attended a meeting of chaplains at which Col. Ross Flemington, Principal Chaplain overseas, addressed us and told the story of the Chaplain Service in France and Western Europe. I also learned from him that Chap. George Harris had been killed in the paratroop landings in Normandy on D-Day. George and I had been acquaintances since the summer of 1931, my first in Holy Orders, and I had supported his entry into the ministry.

That same New Year's Eve I also learned that I had been detailed to go to a Chaplain's Refresher Course being held at Assisi under the auspices of the 8th Army, commencing January 4, 1945. I realized this was a further collaborative move by Al Saunders and Frank Hiltz to get me out of the forward area before a shell or a bullet found its mark and I became history. I appreciated their forethought and organized myself to leave on Tuesday, January 2, 1945, for the long drive through the mountains to Assisi.

Passing through divisional headquarters, I called in to report to McKinney, our Senior Chaplain. He asked me if I would consent to a transfer some time in the near future, to which I replied that I was quite happy to continue with the West Novas, but was ready to serve anywhere I was sent. Reflecting upon this conversation, I was relieved to know that the change Colonel Saunders had spoken of prior to his leaving the regiment was under consideration. During my eleven months with the West Novas I had seen far too much of blood, wounds, and death, and I longed for the day when I could say goodbye to it all and return home to my family.

Continuing our journey, my driver and I called in at No. 1 Canadian General Hospital at Jesi, only to learn that heavy snowdrifts blocked the road to the south. I had supper at the mess and spent the evening visiting the wards, where I located four of our officers who had recently been wounded: Maj. Bill David, Captains Johnson, McGillivray, and Jordan, and Lieutenant Miller from the Westminster Regiment. Continuing our journey the following morning we were turned back at Fabriano because the road was still blocked with snow. After a further visit with Bill David, I spent the evening in the mess at No. 1 Canadian General Hospital, where I had a most interesting conversation with a British doctor, Major Erven, who had flown in from Yugoslavia, where he was in charge of Medical Services for the Special Service Force. They had been working with the Partisans, preparing for an abortive Allied push into Austria to forestall the Russian advance into Austria and eastern Germany.

Having been turned back from the blocked pass on Thursday, we set out from Fabriano early on Friday, January 5, to get ahead of the traffic that we knew would be heavy. We were stopped for two hours at a five-mile stretch of road that had been reduced to a single lane with snow piled high on either side. At the far end of this narrow strip the traffic was lined up for three miles, but we arrived at Assisi at 1500 hours and got nicely settled in before afternoon tea.

The course was held in a delightful old medieval inn called the Minerva, which featured a comfortable sitting room and a beautiful little chapel for quiet and prayer. At evensong we had the first address, which set out the aim of the course as "refreshment," as introduced by the words of Jesus in Matthew 11:28–30: "Come to me, all you that are weary and carrying heavy burdens, and I will give you rest. Take my yoke upon you, and learn from me; for I am gentle and humble in heart, and you will find rest for your souls. For my yoke is easy, and my burden is light." The leader of the conference, the Reverend Robin Wood, later Dean of Windsor, applied the message of the Master to the needs of the men gathered together for these few days of quiet reflection, each of whom had been seeking to meet the spiritual needs of the men of the 8th Army, who were immersed in some of the most bloody battles of the war.

Our program during the weekdays commenced at 0730 hours with matins and Holy Communion, followed at 0945 hours by a Bible Study and discussion. In the early afternoon we were free to read and relax in our rooms, or, if we wished, to go on conducted tours, under Robin's leadership, of sites and areas associated with the life of St. Francis. At 1700 hours Major Brown introduced discussions on "The Church and the Soldier," followed by evensong and address. After supper we played "Consequences" and other games, following which we had more informal discussion and reminiscences of happenings in our Units.

Our last Bible Study and discussion was on the Life Everlasting. Throughout the five days we had been pondering our varied responsibilities on behalf of the men who had to press on with their grim task until the enemy had been driven to surrender. Now, however, we were called to consider the state of those men and women who had given their lives in this struggle. For answers we were called to a consideration of the teaching of Jesus on this subject, to the accounts of the resurrection of Jesus on the first Easter day, as found in the final chapters of each of the Four Gospels, and to the interpretation given by Paul in his letters to first-generation Christians. Christians believe that in our baptism and by our faith in Christ we become a member of Christ, the child of God, and an inheritor of the Kingdom of Heaven, otherwise described as Life Everlasting. In other words, we believe that in Christ we enter into a new dimension of life which is eternal, endless.

The Chaplain's Refresher Course was one of the most spiritually enriching and memorable occasions of my three and a half years of service in the army. I was familiar with such retreats from my ministry in rural Manitoba before the war, but the program at Assisi had the added relevance of being geared particularly to the needs of chaplains ministering to men involved in the chaos of war. The leadership was superb, and I returned to my regiment refreshed and feeling renewed inwardly, ready to cope with the many problems that I realized I would face. Chief among these was the rate of burnout among the officers and men of the West Nova Scotia Regiment. They sorely needed the rest that I had just experienced, but there was no way of providing them with it. They would have to simply press on with the task until it was completed.

Back at the Unit, I found it necessary to reorient myself as the company positions were very widely spread out, making it impossible to hold Sunday services. Fortunately, I was able to drive around to each company HQ and arrange for Padre's Hours and communion services during the week. This provided an opportunity for me to chat with each of the company commanders, and I was not happy with what I learned. There was widespread discontent and unhappiness and there was far too much drinking. Conversation with company officers prior to my departure for Assisi had led me to hope that the regiment was settling down under its new leadership, but this was not so, and I realized it was important for me to take time with the men, to hear them out, and discuss the situation with them.

On Monday, January 15, I had a talk with the CO, now Lieutenant Colonel Hiltz, about these problems, Being very careful to maintain confidentiality, I alerted him to the discontent and especially the drinking, and the effect these would have should the regiment undertake any action. I found the CO very much aware of the problems and ready to discuss ways of coping. I arranged to hold a series of Padre's Hours with the men, in groups of platoon strength wherever possible, about "Five Points for Peace" that were being suggested by Christian leaders as necessary to the building of a better world after the war.

The Five Points for Peace were, first, abolition of extreme inequalities in wealth and possessions; second, equal opportunity of education; third, protection of the family as a social unit; fourth, restoration of the sense of divine vocation to men's and women's daily work; and fifth, a determination to use the earth's resources as God's gift to the whole human race.

Needless to say, my presentations elicited lively discussion that was, for the most part, constructive. However, one group of forty or more refused to keep to the point of the discussion, so we did not get through the questions as I had planned. I reflected that they had let off a lot of steam and would perhaps feel better as a consequence, and I resolved that the next time I met with them I would get right down to business with their real problem—themselves and self-pity, which is the most destructive form of selfishness and makes men unfit for any job. The regiment was not in good shape. So many of the old hands were done in and weary and in need of a thorough rest and reconditioning. New men coming in under those conditions became infected with their spirit and were spoiled before they began, so much so that the NCOs did not feel they had their men behind them when they went out to do a job.

About this time we received word that a major move was in the offing, and I received a gift of an excellent accordion from our Scout, a Newfoundland native named Charlie Fleet. This was placed in my care, to be transported in my truck since its owner had no way of carrying it in his gear. Realizing we were going to be in need of music for our services once we left Russi, I tried playing it and was surprised to discover that with a little more practice I would be able to work out some hymns.

Back in the line again, northwest of Bagnacavalo, on Sunday, January 21, I arranged a number of services and, it being the third Sunday after epiphany, decided I should speak on the Gospel of Matthew, in which a roman soldier believes that Jesus can heal his servant and Jesus, marveling at the soldier's faith, does so.

My first two services were sparsely attended, even though there was no action to consume the men's attention. Out at D Company the service was packed, and it was attended by the company commander and several platoon officers along with other ranks. Where there is interest at the top there is interest all down the line, and it was interest, not compulsion, that brought them. I had a lunch of chicken in broth with Lieutenant Hollinger's platoon and remained afterwards while he briefed his men—a map and situation report—on the positions and work of patrols the night before. If all platoon officers were like this one we would have had a better army and more satisfied men.

That evening a private dropped in at the regimental aid post—drunk. He had been at the service at main battalion HQ in the morning and had he presented himself for Communion, which I administered. When I asked him what was the matter, the poor man said he just wanted to speak with me. I believe he really wanted the help of God, but he was a victim of long-established habits that ruled his life. He told me he had tried to make a fresh start before Christmas and had been drinking much less. But now, evidently, his friends had made fun of him or, quite probably, jibed him about his conduct being unworthy of one who partakes in such a service. He had taken it to heart and gone out and got drunk. That night he was down and needed help. He knelt and prayed to God to cleanse him and make him worthy, and promised to see me the next morning. Then, to my astonishment, he begged the MO to give him a tot of rum. God's help would be needed in abundance to restore his self-respect and manhood.

On Tuesday morning, January 23, I set out with my batman, Jack, to visit A Company, where we remained for lunch. I visited the anti-tank and machine-gun positions along the way, then walked over to C Company and had a visit with them in a strongly reinforced house. Then it was on to B Company, which we knew was under observation from the dikes at the river, but the enemy did not fire much in the daytime and we were unmolested. It was not possible to visit the forward platoons as they did not want people walking around in daylight. The irony of the army! I visited the reserve platoon of A Company under Scotty. There, morale was high, as the men expected to go to Bagnacavalo on leave and Scotty was about to depart for a course. However, when I visited their company headquarters the plans had changed. They were given a fighting patrol task to take out enemy positions on the other side of the river, an extremely dangerous undertaking. On my way back I noticed its gloomy effect on the men. To go on day leave at first light, straight from a patrol, having had no sleep at all, would be heartbreaking.

Lieutenant Clements invited me to a chicken dinner at his Anti-Tank Platoon HQ. We sat down with an Italian family at a huge table spread with a white tablecloth, dishes, and all the trimmings, even bowls of oranges—a most happy gathering. The Italian men sat with their hats on, evidently a local custom. When the younger Italian men saw that we had taken off our berets, they removed their hats, too. Except the grandpa. He was determined to uphold the custom! After supper I had a long chat with Lieutenant Clements about Christianity, the hope of the world, and the power of a spiritual bond in marriage. A few weeks later he discussed with me the possibility of his training for the ministry after the war. He had been brought up in a strict Baptist family, but had reacted against it all and thought he was an atheist. By reading C.S. Lewis's books he had grasped an image of God as love and this enabled him to believe that God was with him and was calling him to offer himself for training for the ministry in the Anglican Church. I encouraged him to press on with those plans.

On Thursday afternoon I went with Lieutenant McKinnon and a party of eleven men to practice a patrol on the banks of the Lamone. It was most enlightening to see him direct his men. He placed the two Bren gunners in the rear flanks to give covering fire, with the others well spread out. It looked like the kickoff in a football match. The men scrambled up and over the embankment, each knowing his position and task. Then, with the two men on the flanks protecting the soldiers with covering fire, the rest of the patrol went through to capture a prisoner. In the debriefing that followed they were reminded that there could be no hitches, that no one could get excited and no one could drop out. Each man depended on the others to do their part. When they came out, they would all come out, wounded or not. So no one needed to fear he would be left behind. Seven men had volunteered for this patrol, one of whom was a Native Indian lad who had volunteered for every patrol that went out.

On Sunday, January 28, I held a service for 3rd Field Company of the Royal Canadian Engineers. On arrival, I found a very penitent group of men. They had been proud of the job they had done in carrying a Bailey bridge approximately one hundred miles on top of two tanks, and setting it up without delay across the Lamone River, allowing the armour to cross in support of the Infantry advance. The Engineers were congratulated on the speed with which they had responded to the challenge left by the retreating enemy, who had blown up the bridge over the Lamone before departing. The new crossing had accordingly been named Mission Bridge. But three weeks later, with the bridge in constant use, a man who was clearing up some of the wreckage of the old bridge accidentally set off a charge beneath the new one and blew it up. Hence the Engineers' penitence when I met them that morning. They informed me they had renamed the rebuilt structure Remission Bridge.

My reading for Monday, January 29, was Mark, chapter 9, and I spent some time reflecting upon verses 30 and 31: "And they departed thence, and passed through Galilee; and he would not that any man should know it. For he taught his disciples, and said unto them, 'The Son of man is delivered into the hands of men, and they shall kill him; and after that he is killed, he shall rise the third day.'" Was this not what had happened to the youth of our generation? They had been betrayed by their elders and teachers into the hands of men. The rich and the powerful, unwilling to reconsider their ways, drove us on into this. Who pays the price? The young and the innocent, these lads who were too young to have had any influence at the time the war was brewing. Therein lay the greatest wickedness of selfishness and greed and lust for power—that the men who make wars and profit by them do not do the fighting. Their very wealth protects them; they buy themselves off by getting into positions of influence, where they are protected from the bullets, and are in a position to better themselves at the expense of the lifeblood of the nation. It is the old, old story of the rich and the privileged sending the Son of man to the cross. There is always a barbarian handy to carry out their dastardly wishes, whether he is a Pontius Pilate, as in the case of Jesus, or a Hitler, as in our generation. There is no escaping the guilt. Pilate and Hitler are both guilty of atrocities before God and man, but it is also true that "he that handed me over to you hath the greater guilt." Those men who stood by and allowed this situation to develop are the truly guilty ones.

The CO, Lt. Col. Frank Hiltz, in an effort to deal fairly with men who had ongoing problems, introduced a custom of inviting me to sit in as an observer at his Office Hours, when he interviewed men up on charges. In some cases he deferred judgement until later and then discussed the case with me in private. On occasion, when I could not be present, he forwarded a sealed package, containing a number of charge sheets of men whose problems I was familiar with. After pondering these I would return them in a sealed envelope, and arrange to see him at my earliest convenience. I felt Frank was doing his best to cope with the problems that he had inherited. The men had been too long away from home and it was difficult to meet their needs in our situation.

On Friday, February 2, I drove out to B Company and conferred with the company commander, Major McAdam, about the problems being experienced by three of his men. I met them at No. 11 Platoon, interviewed each, and had supper with them. I returned for further consultation with the company commander and later I passed along my impressions and suggestions for resolving the problems to the CO. One man's problem was solved by transferring him into the machine gunners under Capt. C. Henderson Smith.

When at headquarters on February 4, Dusty Rhodes came up for a visit. He was not well, but when Capt. Walter Garber announced that his promotion to major came through, Dusty cut off his crowns and gave them to Walter, a symbolic act that reminded me of the ascension of Elijah. Dusty had been the spirit of D Company and his mantle fell upon Walter, who would carry his majority well.

Friday, February 9, was moving day. We changed areas with the Loyal Edmonton Regiment and moved back into Russi. My room was on the third floor of the building that the regimental aid post occupied. Just as I got nicely settled, Captain Bent dropped in. He was returning to Canada on leave with sixteen other ranks who had served with the regiment since 1939. At last, these and others were being posted to a well-earned leave home. At this time the regiment also received reinforcements of one officer and 118 other ranks. The CO, Lt. Col. Frank Hiltz, went on a short leave and Maj. John Cameron succeeded to temporary command of the regiment. Cameron attended the 8th Army Commanders' Conference at Rimini, where the attending officers were pledged to secrecy with the information that the Canadian Corps was about to leave Italy to become part of the Canadian Army in the final battles of the war in northwestern Europe. Our fighting in Italy was finished!

After lunch I arranged to have the Dome Theatre for Sunday services. On arriving at my office in the late afternoon, Jack Garland leaned out a top window and called, "Hey Padre! Did you see your brother?" "What do you mean, my brother?" I replied, "I don't have a brother out here." "Yes, you do. He's in the Princess Pats and they are in that big warehouse a street over having supper before they go into the line. If you go over now you will be able to see him before they leave." So, over I went, and sure enough, there was my brother, Archie, in the chow line with his mess tins. I had a few words with him before he went in to supper and I hoped to bring him out for a short visit on Monday.

When the war broke out, Archie had been working in a gold mine at Little Long Lac in Northern Ontario, and had responded to an appeal for hard rock miners to join the Engineers. He had been sent overseas early in the war and was engaged in building roads strong enough to withstand the wear and tear of heavy armoured vehicles. He was not entirely happy in this occupation, and when an appeal went out for volunteers for the infantry serving in Italy, he responded and was taken on by the Princess Pats serving on the Adriatic Front. I was involved in preparing for the dedication of our cemetery during the following week, but on February 20, the CO loaned me his jeep and driver and I went up to Bagnacavalo to see my brother, only to learn he had been wounded when out on a night patrol on February 13. I went to the casualty collecting post and the advanced dressing station, and from there to the 58th British Field Dressing Station at Ravenna, but he had been sent on down and was listed as a casualty at No. 1 Canadian General Hospital at Jesi. I drove back, disheartened at not finding my brother.

On Wednesday, February 21, Honorary Major McKinney, the divisional chaplain, came for lunch and Ernie MacQuarrie, chaplain to the Carleton and Yorks, joined us afterwards. We went out to the dedication service together. It was a beautiful day and the public relations officers and Maple Leaf staff were on hand to take pictures. The regiment paraded to the service and formed a hollow square around the cemetery, which was located in an apple orchard just south and east of the town of Russi. We had buried our dead here from the bitter fighting for the Russi canal, at the town of Russi, at the Lamone River crossing, up beyond Bagnacavalo, and from patrolling in front of the Senio River, for the period December 2, 1944, to February 10, 1945. There, in that beautiful quiet spot, thirty-four of our men lay buried, including Alex Vingar, MM (awarded for bravery in the Hitler Line battle), Sgt. A.J. Amero, MM (who, as a private soldier in an earlier battle, had saved the lives of comrades in a desperate situation), and Maj. James Harvey Jones, MC (for courageous leadership in the battle for Ortona).

The service was attended by Brigadier Bernatchez; the CO, Lt. Col. Frank Hiltz, who read the address and unveiled the sign board; Honorary Capt. George Hooper, Brigade Roman Catholic chaplain, who offered prayers on behalf of Roman Catholic personnel; and myself, the unit padre, who offered prayers of memorial and dedication on behalf of all Protestant personnel. This was followed by a two-minute silence in remembrance of all the brave men and women who had sacrificed their lives in the campaign from Sicily throughout Italy to the banks of the Senio River. It was a solemn moment which would never be forgotten by those who were present, for we were leaving behind us in Italy the bodies of some of the finest men we had ever known, men whom we had come to know better than our own kith and kin, because we had shared with them the common torment and distress of war and had been with them under all kinds of adversity and danger. It is under conditions like these that the souls of men stand revealed for what they really are.

Immediately after this service, Colonel Hiltz loaned me his jeep and driver and I set out at 1630 hours to locate my brother Archie. After a full day's drive I located him, approximately 150 miles south in No. 11 British General Hospital. He was looking well following surgery for a wound in the abdomen. Shrapnel had entered his right side and gone up almost to his solar plexus, but it had not damaged any internal organs. The doctors assured him he would be all right. I had a longer visit with him the following day and he told me more about how it had happened. He was out on a night patrol on a very dark night and a man next to him tripped an "S" mine, a type that springs up about five feet in the air and explodes, sending ball bearings in all directions. Fortunately, he heard the familiar hissing noise it makes when tripped, and immediately turned to his left. The shrapnel entered his side and lodged on a rib, just below the heart. He was left in a bad way, but managed to crawl out. It was with much relief that I was able to send a telegram to Mother, stating that I had visited him and he would be home in due time.

While preparing for our move across Italy, I held another series of Padre's Hours with the men. My subject was "Marriage" and the men listened with rapt attention for a full hour. I stressed the meaning of the relationship and its enrichment of the lives of the couple, how they were to give themselves to each other in love and faithfulness. I reminded them of the tremendous work of readjustment that we would all face with our wives and families when we returned home. Our prayers would assist us on that great day just as their prayers had sustained us as we tackled our grim tasks throughout the past six years.

And so our sojourn in Italy came to an end.

Chapter Twelve

Liberating Holland
February 27 – May 8, 1945
Italy / England / France / Holland

On Tuesday, February 27, plans for our move having been finalized and all preparations made for our journey, I set out, driving south through Ravenna, down the sun route to Porto San Recanati and to No. 11 British Hospital in the hope of a visit with Archie, but he had already been flown out to a convalescent hospital. I spent the night there and on the following day drove on down to Porto San Giorgio, where our advance party had billets all arranged. We remained there for ten days, and I was kept busy holding Padre's Hours and Sunday services and interviewing soldiers. One important conversation I had was with with Corporal Johnson, who declared he was an atheist and found no need for God in his life. I shared with him my early experience as an unbeliever who found God by taking a simple step of faith. I loaned him C.S. Lewis's book, *Beyond Personality*.

I attended a dinner for NCOs at D Company and had a very enjoyable evening. The men, being definitely out of the line, seemed more open to express their thoughts. Their cook, Cpl. Murray McNeil, informed me he had thought for the past year that I held against him the fact that he had used some bad language within my hearing at Villa Grande the previous year. I had borne him no such grudge, and I was very glad he allowed this to surface to get it off his mind. The following day I had another interview with Corporal Johnson, who returned the book, *Beyond Personality*. He enjoyed reading it and was really pondering the whole question of a deeper dimension to living.

In the afternoon I joined D Company in a scheme carried out through hilly country. Brigadier Bernatchez joined us, and I was particularly interested in his criticisms and suggestions. On one segment of the exercise, when the troops were moving forward in battle formation and then falling prone at regular intervals over terrain with a fairly steep downward slope, the brigadier called on me to give my impressions of what had I had witnessed. My reply was that it was a fundamental mistake to stop and go down on a slope facing the enemy for, in doing so, they were making themselves sitting ducks, and would immediately be shot by the enemy. The brigadier agreed, and he gave the young officer a lecture.

On Monday, March 12, we set out again, drove north to Civitanova, west to Foligno, then north again through the Umbrian plains, passing by Assisi and Arezzo and stopping for the night just outside Florence, the city of Boccaccio, Petrarch, and Michelangelo. On the following morning we set out early and crossed the Arno within sight of the Ponte Vecchio, the only bridge not destroyed completely.

Driving along on the southern escarpment of the Arno, I became fascinated by the river. Periodically, tributaries flowed in from the north or south, and a section of the river changed in colour, depending on the countryside through which it had flowed. The river gradually became absorbed into the larger body of water flowing out to the ocean. Reflecting upon this, I thought of the various branches of the Christian Church, each bringing its particular contribution to the flow of life and each in turn becoming a part of that stream of life that flows from the throne of God into the life of the world, enriching the lives of men and women. The ordeal of war had brought us together as brothers engaged in a common cause. Would the Church leaders at home be able to accept this vision? Would they be willing to make the sacrifices of material wealth to make possible the building of one world in peace and justice? What a vision! What a task!

We passed within sight of Pisa, and I was able to make out the leaning tower through the haze that overhung the whole plain. Arriving at Harrod's Camp, near Livorno (Leghorn), on the west coast of Italy, I parted company with my truck, which went into the transport park, ready for loading. We remained here for five days, and I was able to hold Padre's Hours and arrange trips for the men and officers, in groups, to visit and climb the leaning tower. In the evening of March 16, the company sergeant majors and the company quartermaster sergeants called on me to have a chat before leaving Italy, and to let me know how much they had appreciated everything I had done for the men while with them in Italy. On Sunday, March 18, I held an open-air service in Livorno forest, the last one I was to conduct in Italy. My subject for that Passion Sunday was "Going up to Jerusalem."

At 1900 hours on Monday, March 19, HQ Company and battalion HQ, moved off in US army trucks, passing through Livorno and down to the harbour where we boarded an LCT (Landing Craft Tank) and sailed out of a harbour cluttered with sunken ships and wreckage. We were not sorry to be leaving Italy behind, and enjoyed our two-day cruise to Marseilles, France. In one hour the ship was completely unloaded and I was on my way to the camp, where I linked up again with my truck. The summer weather was perfect, and I liked the atmosphere of France. Marseilles looked more like Montreal than any city I had seen. We camped about fifteen miles out of Marseilles and got a very early start on the following morning. On our second day we passed through Lyon, where St. Irenaeus laboured as bishop of a small Christian community during the second Christian century, enduring much persecution. On Sunday, March 25, Palm Sunday, we were on the move early. The news was very good; seven Allied armies had crossed the Rhine. After three days of travel we camped just outside of Cambrai, hoping to see Paris, but the sky was overcast and it was raining. Another day brought us into Belgium to Berlaar, where we were billeted in private homes over Good Friday and the Easter weekend.

I had my office above the battalion orderly room and was busy interviewing men and officers, including another discussion with Corporal Johnson. On Good Friday I held a service in the afternoon and gave my reflections on "the men who crucified Christ." Corporal Johnson called in on Saturday morning to say goodbye. He was on his way home to Canada, and came in to thank me for all the help I had given him in our discussions about belief in God, concluding with, "I cannot say that I have arrived yet, but I am now at least seeing some light and shall continue to ponder the question." I received correspondence from this young man after I returned to Canada, reporting that he was married, had returned to become an active member of the church, and had just celebrated the baptism of their first child.

I received a pleasant surprise on Saturday, March 31, in a parcel from the Senior Chaplain at corps HQ, containing the contents of my small pack, which had somehow been sent out from the regimental aid post with a wounded man, and was only now emerging into daylight. It contained my prayer book, a picture of my wife and family, my glasses, tobacco pouch, shaving kit and razor, and a parcel of letters that I had received just before we went into action on that occasion and had not yet read—a very welcome surprise.

On Easter Sunday, April 1, 1945, I held an Easter service. The following Wednesday, April 4, we were off at 0630 hours, passing through southern Holland and camping in the Reichwald Forest for a few days. The evidence of hard fighting was everywhere present, there and across the border as we approached Nijmegen. I called at the Princess Pats to enquire after Archie, but they had received no further word, so I assumed he was out for the duration. While there I held a series of Padre's Hours at which we discussed "Evolution and Religion," which evoked lively discussion. I felt it was touching a chord and helping them to understand the relationship between science and religion as two complementary approaches to reality.

On Monday, April 9, I set out for a ten-day leave, my first in England, along with my batman, Jack Garland. We drove to Nijmegen where we entrained for Calais, took the Channel boat for Folkestone, and arrived in London on Tuesday evening. On Thursday I took the train to Matlock for a visit with Uncle Lew and Aunt Millie Hofton. Aunt Belle, my father's younger sister, joined us for tea.

On Saturday, April 14, I took the train to Northallerton, to see my younger brother Walter, who was at the time a pilot in Bomber Command. We spent Sunday together visiting at York. After another day with Uncle Lew and Aunt Millie in Matlock, I learned from the Chaplain's Office in London that my friend John O. Anderson, chaplain with the Grenadiers Guards, a light tank regiment, was seriously wounded and had been flown to No. 2 Canadian Hospital at Bramshott. I took the train to Hazelmere and caught a ride up to the hospital, where I spent the afternoon visiting quietly with him. His jeep had been blown up by teller mines while taking him to a funeral after the capture of Almelo, in northeastern Holland. Both his legs and his right arm were in casts, and he had been badly shaken up. It was good to see him and I think he was cheered by my visit. I prayed with him at his bedside before going on my way.

The full story of John's accident came out only in 1993, when I was on one of Don Morgan's tours of northwestern Europe, with Brig. Gen. Patrick Grieve (rtd.) serving as military instructor and consultant to the tour. We arrived at Almelo, and Patrick described for us the battle at the conclusion of which John was wounded. Grieve was a captain, serving as adjutant. The Guards captured the village after a bitter running battle, but as they moved over the canal into the centre of the town one of their tanks was fired on from the upper floor of a tall house facing the canal, killing both pilot and co-pilot and setting the tank on fire. The bodies of the two men were sitting upright in the tank and had to be removed without delay. The driver of the jeep was not available, having been sent on some much-needed leave, and the adjutant, Patrick, agreed to drive the padre, John.

Having removed the bodies from the tank and wrapped them in blankets, they were digging graves beside the canal when some Dutch people came out and insisted that these men, as heroes who had liberated their town, must be buried in consecrated ground. There was a cemetery just over the canal and down one block to the left. They would go and prepare the graves while the padre obtained what he needed to conduct the burial. There were two Boy Scouts on hand who would go with the padre and guide the driver to the cemetery.

All went well until the jeep turned off the street onto the road leading into the cemetery. Here it crossed what appeared to be a shallow wooden bridge, but was actually a row of five teller mines placed under boards. A single teller mine could blow a hole in the floor of a jeep and severely wound its occupants, but in this case the jeep was blown sky high, the driver thrown forward to the left, the padre to the right, and both Boy Scouts backwards to right and left. The military personnel were picked up and rushed to hospital, and then flown to England for emergency attention. The two Boy Scouts were taken to a local hospital where they were examined, one being retained for a couple of weeks, but the other sent home, with only a few bruises, to tell his story. Patrick Grieve and John Anderson both recovered from their serious wounds, but they had received no information about what had become of the two boys. To our very great surprise, while we were enjoying lunch in a restaurant in Almelo on September 28, 1993, a professor from a local college brought in the two men who had been the Boy Scouts, and we had the joy of witnessing the meeting of these three men who hadn't seen each other in decades. They greeted one another like those who had arisen from the grave, for the boys had not known whether the two officers had lived, and Patrick had assumed that the boys must have been killed, for the jeep was totally demolished. It was a rare privilege to be present at such a meeting after all those years, and that luncheon at Almelo was the high point of a most enjoyable tour.

To return to my visit to Bramshott, I remained at the hospital overnight, and learned from an arranged broadcast over the radio that my Channel crossing had been delayed by twenty-four hours, giving me another day. Being aware that Dr. Geoffrey Fisher was being enthroned as Archbishop of Canterbury on April 19, I took the train and went down to be present for that event in the life of the Church. I was unable to get inside the cathedral, but had a very good view of the procession as the Archbishop proceeded out the great west doors. After the service I spent an hour walking about the cathedral, which bears the marks of so much of England's history. The school and library were both demolished by bombs, but the fine old building escaped with but a few scars.

I took the train to London and from there to Folkestone, where I spent the night and caught the ferry to Calais in the morning, arriving at Nijmegen after a day spent on a slow train. The West Novas had been in action for the past week, had liberated Apeldoorn, and pushed north and west to the south shore of the Zuider Zee, where we located the Rear Battalion at Nijkerk. We settled in for a good night's sleep, but before going to bed I learned that Frank Hiltz was being relieved of his command and would be leaving us. The officers held a farewell party for him on Sunday evening and we said goodbye to Frank at lunch on Monday.

On Monday afternoon our new CO, Lt. Col. J. Aird Nesbit, arrived and I had a good chat with him in my truck. I found him to have a strong and pleasing personality with plenty of drive, and reckoned he would have no difficulty in getting the very best out of everyone under his command. The Saskatchewan Light Infantry across the road had an accident with a German stick grenade, which wounded six army and six civilian personnel. I helped bandage them up and took them to the regimental aid post. Private MacLennan, a signalman, was wounded by shellfire in A Company area. He lost a leg, but otherwise was in good shape. Private Drapeau was killed by shellfire. I went to Nijkerk to arrange for the burial in the local cemetery, and notified Padre Hooper, who came up and took charge of the burial.

During the last week in April it was evident to all that the war in Europe could not go on much longer, in fact, no more than a few days at the most. The Allied forces had broken through on all fronts and the Russians were breaking into Berlin. Hitler's attention was taken up with his own ritual immolation before the Russians captured him alive. Fortress Holland had been isolated, cutting off all escape routes for the 125,000 coastal defence troops. The 1st Canadian Division, having thrust north to the Zuider Zee, now swung west towards the Eem River with Amsterdam as our apparent objective. The West Novas had exchanged places with the Carleton and Yorks and were now spread out in a long line from Ham to the Zuider Zee. HQ was at Langenoord, from which we could see quite plainly the great church tower in Amersfoort, which, it was suspected, was being used as an observation post by the enemy. While discussions were underway as to whether or not to shell the tower, a new development brought a reprieve.

On April 25, General Blaskowitz, commander of the German troops defending Fortress Holland, notified General Montgomery that he would permit Allied food trucks to pass through the lines in order to bring emergency food to the starving people of The Hague and other beleaguered cities. A five-day truce was agreed upon commencing April 26, during which all army personnel were ordered to remain in positions, but not to engage the enemy unless fired upon. Strict orders were issued to all ranks that there was to be no unnecessary movement about the area.

Despite this truce, the Germans on our immediate front continued to machine-gun and mortar our forward troops throughout 27 and 28 April, and one of our men, Private Fitzgerald, died of his wounds while being brought out to the regimental aid post. On May 2, the CO was informed that the truce was over, but that he must not engage in any offensive action. There followed a period of watchful waiting for two more days. On Friday, May 4, our front was quiet, even though the truce was officially over. Our people had been instructed to refrain from firing unless fired upon. Queen Wilhelmina and her cabinet in London had urged the British High Command to refrain from attacking Fortress Holland during a period when it was believed that the German High Command was seriously considering surrender. This resulted in a one-way truce, for the German forces opposing us, including at one point a troop of Dutch Nazi soldiers, were determined they were going to capture a Canadian. Fortunately, the Canadians were alert and the attack was driven off with no casualties to us.

With orders to refrain from going about the area, I took advantage of the situation and used the opportunity to brush up my knowledge of Greek in preparation for post-war studies in divinity. I also continued my interviews with the soldiers, and when I had occasion to go to the CO about one case, I found Aird Nesbit to be a most generous and understanding leader of men, one who responded readily to solve problems when possible. There continued to be men in the regiment who had been away from their families for three to four years, and their problems were increasing as the war dragged on. But the moment that we had all been awaiting arrived by way of a BBC news flash at 2030 hours, on May 4, when regimental radio picked up the following announcement: "Allied Supreme Headquarters announces that the German forces in northwest Germany, Holland, and Denmark have surrendered unconditionally to Field Marshal Montgomery's 21st Army Group. Surrender to become effective 8 a.m., May 5th."

The German armies in Italy had surrendered on April 26 and Hitler, unable to face the humiliation of defeat and the judgement of history, had committed suicide in his bunker in Berlin on April 30. Now the battle lines in Fortress Holland fell silent. Yet our troops continued to man their various posts in the line for another two days while the details of the surrender were worked out. On the afternoon of May 5, General Blaskowitz signed the formal papers of surrender to Lt. Gen. Charles Foukes, commander of the 1st Canadian Corps. The war on our front was over.

On Monday, May 7, I went out on a bicycle to visit A and D Companies. At breakfast we received word that the war would be over as of midnight, and the CO called an orders group in which we learned that we would set off at 0530 hours on the following morning to move, not to Amsterdam, where they expected we might go, but to an area near The Hague, with a four-battalion brigade, including the 48th Highlanders—a three-hour trip, with haversack rations and no halts on the way. As we neared the city the Dutch people went wild with excitement to see the Canadians coming. They mobbed our trucks each time we stopped at a crossroads and wanted us to come over and shoot the German soldiers who were still standing guard at anti-aircraft stations. A scout car had preceded us, planting the "TAC 69" signs clearly at each crossroad to make sure no mistakes were made as to direction. But some enthusiastic welcomer moved the sign directing us past The Hague to Delft, and instead directed part of our convoy into The Hague, where we were hailed as the liberators of Holland. The Dutch, excited as they were, could scarcely understand the situation. For, at the roadside, as we momentarily stopped, there were German soldiers manning anti-aircraft guns, yet we paid no attention to them. In the city we were besieged by Dutch underground men in overalls with pistols stuck in their belts, who wanted us to come with them and capture Germans who were still occupying certain buildings.

Our trucks were completely mobbed by cheering young people and for a time all efforts at clearing them failed. I was aware that our section of the convoy had become split off and we were lost until I finally located the railway station, where I contacted a man who rode out with us and led our section of the convoy out to Delft, our destination. Here I located brigade HQ, and was directed to Den Hoorn, where I was billeted in the home of the school headmaster. Despite our detour, we arrived shortly after noon and were settled in time to hear Prime Minister Winston Churchill come on the BBC and announce the end of the war in Europe. My host, the headmaster, brought out a special bottle of wine, a *Petit Bourgogne,* which he had kept for this occasion, and we drank to the future as Churchill spoke.

Chapter Thirteen

The Guns Fall Silent
May 9 – August 15, 1945
Holland / England / Canada

On the morning of Wednesday, May 9, I drove into Delft with the MO to find a church for a service of thanksgiving. We located a large Gothic building that had been taken over by the Dutch Reformed Church. The great sanctuary now contained the tomb of William the Silent where at one time the altar had stood. We felt this would be an ideal location for our service, but on return to our base we discovered the unit was on the move again and all our plans were cancelled. We drove around The Hague to the suburb of Voorburg, where we took over a large mansion that had until recently been occupied by a German general and his staff. It now became our rear battalion.

Before I got really settled there, we moved yet again. Our troops were very much spread out, busy disarming prisoners and bringing them into a barbed-wire compound in a green belt between The Hague and Scheveningen. Here they gathered sixty thousand of the coastal defence troops, in preparation for their return to Germany. At this point Battalion HQ was established in a large mansion on the main street of Scheveningen, and I had an office where I was available to all personnel.

While this task was being carried out all officers and other ranks in the army were also presented with a further decision about their futures. The chaplains also received a questionnaire asking us to express our preference now that hostilities in Europe had ceased: Did we wish to volunteer for the Canadian Army Pacific Force and become part of a vast army dedicated to the task of invading the Japanese Islands and ending the war in the Pacific? Or did we wish to become a part of the Army of Occupation? Did we wish to return home and take our discharge and return to civilian life? My one wish, after fifteen months of ministering to infantry engaged in the bloody battles in Italy, was to take my discharge, go home, and return to civilian ministry. I said so in my response. We were reminded in the letter accom-

Chapter Thirteen

panying the questionnaire that it would be necessary to have sufficient leadership from men who had seen action in the European conflict, and it might not be possible for our wishes, whatever they might be, to be granted. I realized that, although I had seen heavy fighting for a prolonged period of time, I had actually been away from Canada for only a little less than two years, but, with hope, I sent off my response.

On Thursday, May 17, the burgomaster of Voorburg held a civic reception to celebrate the liberation of the city, and I was one of ten officers from the battalion present to represent the unit. The burgomaster, the city councillors, and the city fathers, with representatives of the Dutch resistance, were assembled in the town hall, and some very fine addresses were read. The Dutch people's hopes and struggles through the long years of the German occupation contrasted with their deep joy at being able to welcome the Canadians, their liberators.

After the formal ceremony we were ushered into a drawing room where we were served a cup of tea and some cheese and met the burgomaster's wife and family. When we left the town hall a huge crowd had gathered to cheer us. So ended a delightful reception by a people who, in all the formality of their proud ancestry, revealed the depth and genuineness of their gratitude. This made us feel even more that it really was worthwhile to have fought to liberate the Dutch.

In their enthusiasm to express their gratitude, the Domine of the Voorburg church informed me that he had invited the regiment to a great service of thanksgiving on Whitsunday and invited me to take part in the service. The troops, immersed in their task of gathering all the German coastal defence troops, were unable to attend, but they invited me to speak to them and I did so on the implications of the end of the long struggle for all of us, and the hope of building a new world which, by the grace of God, lay before us.

Back at my padre's office on the main street, I had some unusual callers. One afternoon, after watching what seemed an endless stream of prisoners going by on their way to the barbed-wire enclosure, I was surprised to have a visit from a German Lutheran chaplain who had been serving German coastal defence troops. He had come to my office with what he considered two important requests. The first concerned three Red Ensigns, of the size flown on merchant ships, which he had brought with him. They had been manufactured at The Hague at the request of the German military to be used by German gunboats, disguised as merchant ships, patrolling the English Channel. Once close to Allied shipping, the boats would shed their disguise and attack. But these particular flags, the chaplain said, he had personally purchased in The Hague for use in the burial of British and Canadian airmen whose planes failed to make it back to base. The ensigns had been used on many occasions and only for burials, and he hoped I might be able to accept them with this in mind, rather than turn them in. I pointed out to him that I must report them, but would explain the service for which they had been used.

Actually, brigade asked me to send one of the flags to them and retain the other two, which I did. One of these I gave away some years ago for what I thought was an appropriate use, and a few years ago I used the third and final one in the dedication of a memorabilia corner in St. John's Ravenscourt School, Winnipeg. I did so because, on reading the obituary list of airmen from St. John's College School and Ravenscourt School during World War II, it became evident that many of these men were among those fliers reported missing and presumed dead following bombing missions over German, and the flags may very well have been used at the burial of several of these men.

The second request of this chaplain was to ask a favour of me on behalf of the Roman Catholic chaplain in their unit. This Roman Catholic chaplain had lived in a suite of rooms at the top of the large building in Scheveningen that was now being used as residence for West Nova officers. While resident there he was living in a common-law relationship with a young woman. They had been required to vacate the building without prior warning and he had left behind a large number of compromising photographs of himself and this woman. Would I please search the drawers of desks and cupboards in these rooms and destroy any such pictures I located?

I had, as a matter of fact, discovered these pictures when we first checked into the hotel and had collected all that I could locate. If he wished that they be destroyed, I would do so without delay. I had been hoping that he would make contact with me and I could have returned them to him. The pictures indicated that this priest had had a warm human relationship with a good-looking woman his own age during this period of his service.

Another interesting visitor I had was a young Dutchman who introduced himself as John Pronk, the president of a secret society that a group of Dutch theological students had formed when the Germans closed their universities. They called it *Spes Salutis* (Hope of Salvation) and they met every Friday evening for prayer, reading, and conversation to strengthen their faith throughout a very difficult period. Many able-bodied young men had been seized by the Gestapo and carried off to become slave labourers in industries in Germany, where every effort was made to brainwash them into becoming Nazis. The members of *Spes Salutis* became deeply concerned about what was happening to these young men and one of their number, a Mr. J. Dansen, allowed himself to be captured and become a labourer in order to secretly meet with young Dutchmen engaged in the same work. In this way he held secret meetings with them to strengthen their faith. Realizing he was a leader, the authorities kept moving him to other projects and in this way facilitated his secret work. But finally they arrested him and he was found by the Allied advance troops in the Belsen death camp. I attended several meetings of *Spes Salutis* and on my final visit this young man joined them and spoke to us about his experience.

This was a very busy time for me because, in addition to my daily tasks, a great many of the officers and men who had served throughout the Italian campaign were returning to Canada and came to say goodbye. Some came with problems, in particular Cpl. Victor Hall and my former driver, Biggy, for each of whom I was able to arrange a short leave in England to enable them to be married en route to Canada.

Major Gilling, Senior Chaplain of Corps, called a conference of all chaplains under his care on Thursday, May 31, at which he outlined the various types of service now available to us. He thanked us for completing the questionnaire, and requested that we rethink our responses, emphasizing the important leadership we seasoned padres could bring to the chaplains service for the Canadian Army Pacific Forces. Although he sympathized with men who had been away from their families for years and wished to return to Canada, he advised us that if volunteers did not come forward they would have to designate needed leadership.

As the Senior Chaplain said this, he looked directly at me, and I went home to rethink my position. After much thought and prayer, I wrote to him, stating that when the war in Europe came to an end, I was taken in by the general attitude that now it was over and we would go home. I was anxious to get back to my family and rebuild my life, and said so in the questionnaire. But I realized now that the war was not over until Japan was defeated. I volunteered for the duration and, if needed, was prepared to serve in the Far East or wherever my services were required. Within a week I learned that I was being appointed second-in-command of the chaplains service for the Canadian Army Pacific Forces.

Making the decision to volunteer, and knowing that my war wasn't over yet, gave me greater peace of mind, and allowed me to proceed with my busy life of Padre's Hours and thanksgiving services in cooperation with the Dutch Reformed church in Scheveningen. I prepared a commendation card, to be given to men who were going home and wished an introduction to their local church. I also prepared and wrote a letter that I signed and sent to 238 next-of-kin of deceased personnel of the regiment. I addressed platoon-sized groups of men, sharing with them the latest information from the government about rehabilitation for those who were returning to civilian life. Finally, I had an interesting chat with Jack Garland, who served as my batman during our final six months in Italy. Jack and I had some close calls together and I appreciated his devotion and courage. I gave him my right armband to wear when he left for the Pacific, where he planned to serve as a stretcher-bearer.

On Sunday, June 17, the regiment attended a farewell service in the Dutch Reformed church on New Park Laan, where we had a congregation of four hundred soldiers and as many civilians in the balconies. I gave the farewell address.

On Tuesday, June 19, having completed its assignment in The Hague, the battalion held a final parade on the square. Col. Aird Nesbitt addressed the troops and called on me to say a few words. The speeches were followed by a march past and salute of the CFEF as they set off to join the Canadian Army Pacific Force on their way to Japan. I spent the next couple of days saying goodbye to all my new friends, and on Thursday we moved to Utrecht where we were located in a large army barracks. While there we saw off another large draft for repatriation to Canada.

On the afternoon of Tuesday, June 26, I attended a meeting of chaplains at divisional HQ, which was attended by Lt. Col. Irwin McKinney, who was now Senior Chaplain. Major Ernie MacQuarrie, erstwhile padre to the Carleton and Yorks, now divisional Senior Chaplain, announced the names of chaplains selected for the CFEF and we had supper together at the Nova Scotian. On Wednesday the West Novas were part of the Guard of Honour when Queen Wilhelmina returned to Amsterdam, and, along with other service officers, I had a good view of her homecoming from an upstairs window across the street from the entrance to her palace.

On July 11, I was transferred out of the regiment and flown to London, England, and on to Blackdown where I linked up with the team of chaplains who had been chosen to serve in the Pacific forces. While there I received my majority and was confirmed in my appointment as second-in-command of the chaplains service. A few days later we boarded the large troop ship, the *Isle de France,* and sailed for Halifax, arriving in August, at about the time the atomic bombs were dropped on Hiroshima and Nagasaki.

After travelling halfway across Canada on a slow train, I arrived home to the welcome of my family after almost two years' absence. That was a tremendous experience for all. My younger daughter, Hope Fairfield, five years of age, spent the afternoon on my knee. The daddy to whom she vaguely remembered waving goodbye almost two years earlier as he marched off with troops through the streets of Brockville, Ontario, had actually materialized, and was present, for a while at least. The apparently temporary nature of my return home was agonizing for the whole family. All about them were families whose men were home to stay. After all, the war in which we had all fought was over. Why, then, must I go off to another similar bloody struggle? People were very good; they did not pester me with questions, but the questions were there in the forefront all the time.

I had ten days' leave and had to make full use of it, so I rented a car and Hope and I drove out to the family farm north of Minnedosa to see my mother, brother, and sisters. We had a pleasant afternoon together and were about to sit down to Sunday dinner when I turned on the radio and learned that the Japanese had surrendered and the war was over. That news was a tremendous relief to me and to everyone in the family. From that moment on I enjoyed my leave. My war was over at last, and I happily turned my thoughts to the challenges of civilian life.

Captain Laurence F. Wilmot at the end of his military duties, 1945.

Glossary

advanced dressing station (ADS)—It was necessary to get seriously wounded soldiers stabilized as soon as possible for transfer to better medical facilities. At the ADS, breathing tubes were inserted, limbs were immobilized, bleeding was suppressed, and antiseptics applied, among many other procedures.

absent without leave (AWOL)—An offence in the services. The penalty depended upon length of absence and theatre of operations.

batman—An officer's personal assistant, who also served as a runner in action.

battalion—A Unit commanded by a lieutenant colonel, consisting of a battalion headquarters, a second-in-command, an adjutant with an orderly room, and the intelligence section; a headquarters company of an administrative platoon including the medical officer in charge of the regimental aid post with medically trained persons, transport personnel, and a signals platoon; a support company of four platoon—three-inch mortars, six-pounder anti-tank, universal Bren gun carriers, and pioneers; and four rifle companies of three platoons, each with three 10-man sections. Each platoon of a rifle company was armed with a two-inch mortar, a PIAT (projector infantry anti-tank), three Bren light machine guns, several sub-machine guns (Thompson or the Sten), rifles, pistols, and grenades. There were three infantry battalions of approximately one thousand men each to a brigade, three brigades to a division, for a total of nine battalions in all.

Bren carrier—Also known as a universal carrier. A lightly armoured tracked vehicle, originally designed to provide protection for a Bren gun and gunner but capable of carrying four to six soldiers and their weapons. It offered overhead protection and had a top speed of thirty-five miles an hour. Some were converted into weapons carriers and played a combat role by being fitted with Vickers .303 medium machine guns, two- or three-inch mortars, and flame-throwers. Some were used to tow the six-pounder anti-tank guns and to evacuate the wounded on stretchers.

brigade—An infantry division had three brigades of three infantry battalions.

Canadian base reinforcement depot (CBRD)—A unit that received reinforcements and sent them forward to fighting units on demand.

casualty collecting post (CCP)—As casualties were recovered from the battlefield they were collected at this central and supposedly safe spot for transport to other medical facilities. The CCP was a triage centre, and not all medical casualties followed the same route. Those requiring urgent medical attention were passed along one route while the less seriously wounded were passed along another.

casualty clearing station (CSS)—A small forward field hospital where serious casualties could receive treatment before being passed back to a base hospital. It contained one or more surgical teams, depending on the casualty estimates for a pending battle.

Canadian Officers Training Corps (COTC)—Most universities had a COTC contingent to train prospective officers during their educational terms.

corporal (CPL)—A rank identifying the leader of a section of ten men.

company quartermaster sergeant (CQMS)—An officer responsible for company rations, supplies of equipment, and other administrative matters.

company sergeant major (CSM)—The senior non-commissioned officer in a company. Responsible for discipline of troops within a company and for the distribution of supplies of rations, ammunition, and other needs of the men.

Carleton and York Regiment from New Brunswick (CYR)—Usually abbreviated to Carleton and Yorks.

field dressing station (FDS)—Used to provide the lightly wounded casualties with necessary medical attention.

forward observation officer (FOO)—An artillery battery had two captains, one in command of the guns and the other a forward observation officer. The forward observation officer would accompany a leading infantry company and establish an observation post with his own radio operator, an important adjunct to company communications. The forward observation officer was in charge of calling for artillery support and directing the fire toward enemy targets that were threatening or holding up the infantry. The battery commander, a major, accompanied the commanding officer and also had his own radio—a doubling of communication in case one radio failed.

The Hastings and Prince Edward Regiment (Hasty Ps)—A regiment from those two counties in Ontario.

headquarters (HQ)—Regardless of size of unit.

Jerry—Common term for Germans. Also spelled Gerry. Canadians seldom used the term Kraut, which was favoured by American soldiers. *Tedeschi*, the Italian word for German, was also popular, as were Hun and Boche.

lieutenant colonel (Lt. Col.)—Often referred to simply as Colonel.

Moaning Minnies—Incoming missiles from a German rocket launcher earned this nickname by their distinctive sound.

non-commissioned officer (NCO)—A lance corporal, corporal, lance sergeant, sergeant, or staff sergeant.

officer commanding (OC)—A commanding officer of a subordinate unit such as an infantry company, artillery battery, or engineer squadron.

orders group (O Gp)—This term refers to the issuing of orders to subordinate commanders who are setting out plans or procedures. Orders start out at the highest level of command and descend downward to the section level. At each step plans are filtered and adjusted to fit subordinate roles. A section commander would receive only those orders pertaining to the successful completion of his section's objective.

Princess Patricia's Canadian Light Infantry (Princess Pats)—A regular force unit from Western Canada.

public relations officer (PRO)—An officer whose job is to interpret the actions of the services into language the general public could understand.

private (Pte.)—A foot soldier, usually an infantryman. The fundamental first rank of a recruit joining the army.

quartermaster (QM)—A regimental officer who controlled most army equipment and supplies such as rations, ammunition, clothing, and other items.

regimental aid post (RAP)—A post set up by the regimental medical officer to give first treatment to casualties.

Royal Canadian Army Service Corps—A corps responsible for supplying forward troops with ammunition, rations, and other equipment.

Royal Canadian Engineers—Responsible for providing many provisions to allow fighting troops to advance in an attack, including bridging, destruction of obstacles such as mines and wire, and many other tasks. In defence they destroy bridges, build anti-tank ditches, string wire, and lay mines, among many other tasks.

Royal Canadian Horse Artillery—Regular force unit that had twenty-four field guns (the basic artillery support for an infantry brigade) but no horses.

Royal Canadian Ordnance Corps—Responsible for the acquisition of equipment, including weapons, clothing, and other amenities.

regiment—A regiment may have several battalions. For instance, the West Nova Scotia Regiment had three during World War II. The first went overseas in 1939 and a second, a militia regiment, was formed to defend its area of influence in Nova Scotia if required. A third was formed to fight in the Pacific in 1945. In the Canadian Army, the words regiment and battalion are often used interchangeably.

Royal Canadian Regiment—A regular force unit from Ontario.

Royal Highland Regiment (The Black Watch)—A regiment with headquarters in Montreal.

regimental quartermaster sergeant—The officer responsible for unit equipment and supplies.

regimental sergeant major—The officer responsible to the CO for discipline within the unit and to forward supplies, especially ammunition, to forward troops.

Royal 22nd Regiment—A regular force unit from Quebec.

Saskatoon Light Infantry (MG)—A unit offering medium machine gun and heavy mortar support.

sergeant—A senior non-commissioned officer, usually the second-in-command of a platoon, with others in charge of specialist sub-units.

second-in-command—The officer responsible for overall administration within the unit or subunit.

S mine—A canister mine of 350 ball bearings packed around a core of explosives. On contact the canister springs five feet above ground and explodes its charge.

Schu mine—A mine consisting of a simple small box of picric acid designed to blow off limbs.

tactical headquarters—A commanding officer had two headquarters, a rear battalion HQ that looked after all administration details and a forward HQ that looked after the tactical situation. They were separated to allow the CO to direct the battle as far forward as deemed safe, and to relieve him of administrative burdens.

West Nova Scotia Regiment—Usually referred to as West Novas. The West Novas, Carleton and Yorks, and Royal 22nd Regiment, formed the 3rd Canadian Infantry Brigade.

Life Writing Series

In the **Life Writing Series,** Wilfrid Laurier University Press publishes life writing and new life-writing criticism in order to promote autobiographical accounts, diaries, letters, and testimonials written and/or told by women and men whose political, literary, or philosophical purposes are central to their lives. **Life Writing** features the accounts of ordinary people, written in English, or translated into English from French or the languages of the First Nations or from any of the languages of immigration to Canada. **Life Writing** will also publish original theoretical investigations about life writing, as long as they are not limited to one author or text.

Priority is given to manuscripts that provide access to those voices that have not traditionally had access to the publication process.

Manuscripts of social, cultural, and historical interest that are considered for the series, but are not published, are maintained in the **Life Writing Archive** of Wilfrid Laurier University Library.

Series Editor
Marlene Kadar
Humanities Division, York University

Manuscripts to be sent to
Brian Henderson, Director
Wilfrid Laurier University Press
75 University Avenue West
Waterloo, Ontario, Canada N2L 3C5